DR. SEBI TREATMENT AND CURES BOOK:

DR. SEBI CURE FOR STDS, HERPES, HIV, DIABETES, LUPUS, HAIR LOSS, KIDNEY, AND OTHER DISEASES

M.S. GREGER

TABLE OF CONTENTS

INTRODUCTION

"A healthy body is worth more than any dollar amount. You don't want to be the wealthiest person on a hospital bed." – Dr. Sebi

Congratulations on taking the first steps to improve your health by choosing Dr. Sebi Treatment and Cures Book. In this book, you will learn all of the healing secrets of Dr. Sebi and how they can help you to improve your health.

Throughout this book, we will discuss the various treatment methods laid out by Dr. Sebi to help you recover from STDs, diabetes, hair loss, lupus, and kidney disease. But before we jump into that information, let's take a look at who Dr. Sebi is.

"Healing has to be consistent with life itself. If it isn't, then it is not healing. The components have to be from life." – Dr. Sebi

Dr. Sebi was born as Alfredo Darrington Bowman on November 26, 1933, in Illanga, Honduras. His grandmother taught him about herbal healing. He was self-educated. Dr. Sebi is considered a naturalist, biochemist, herbalist, and pathologist. Over his years, he studied herbs all over North, Central, and South America, Caribbean, and Africa. He developed and unique methodology and approach to healing humans with herbs that are rooted in more than 30 years of experience.

When he moved to the US, he wasn't happy with the modern medical practices that they used to treat things like impotency, diabetes, and asthma. He had been diagnosed with obesity, impotence, diabetes, and asthma, and had undergone many modern medical treatments that did not help him. That's what led him to an herbalist in Mexico, and shortly thereafter, he started his herbal healing practice in New York.

He eventually started a second practice, which he called the USHA Research Institute, in La Ceiba, Honduras. He worked with many well-known celebrities, including Michael Jackson, Eddie Murphy, John Travolta, Steven Seagal, and Lisa Lopes.

Dr. Sebi dedicated more than 30 years of his life to come up with a methodology that he was only able to come up with through years of empirical knowledge. Inspired by all of his own healing knowledge and experience he had learned, he started to share the compounds with other people. This is how he gave birth to Dr. Sebi's Cell Food.

Dr. Sebi passed away on August 9, 2016, from pneumonia.

"Growth is painful, change is painful, but nothing is as painful as staying the same." – Dr. Sebi

Disclaimer

Please note that we are not doctors and we do not claim to be. We simply follow the instructions of Dr. Sebi.

CHAPTER 1

THE DR. SEBI TREATMENT

The research of Western medicine has stated that diseases are caused by a person being infected by bacteria, viruses, or germs. To help a person overcome this "infestation," doctors provide them with inorganic chemicals. Dr. Sebi's research found the flaws in this premise through simple deductive reasoning. Western medicine has consistently used these same methods, and they have always provided people with the same ineffective results.

Instead, if we look at the African approach to diseases, it opposes Western medicine. The African Bio-mineral Balance rejects the bacteria, virus, and germ theory. Dr. Sebi's research found that diseases are able to grow when the mucous membrane is compromised. For example, if your bronchial tubes have too much mucus, the person is diagnosed with bronchitis. If the mucus is in the lungs, then they have pneumonia. When it moves to the pancreatic duct, they have diabetes. All of the compounds in the African Bio-mineral Balance are made up of natural plants, which make it alkaline.

This is very important in reversing these pathologies because diseases are only able to live in acidic environments. It doesn't make sense to use inorganic compounds to treat diseases because they are acidic. The consistent use of natural remedies will detoxify and cleanse a diseased body and will bring it back to its alkaline state.

Dr. Sebi's nutrition system takes things a step further. Besides getting rid of years of toxin build-up, the African Bio-mineral Balance will replace all of the depleted minerals and will rejuvenate any cell tissue that has been damaged by acid. The main organs that it helps are the colon, kidneys, lymph glands, gall bladder, liver, and skin. When the toxins are released from one of these organs, they will move through the body and manifest in disease. Eventually, the body will start to attack the weakest organ because it is unable to get rid of the toxin. The colon is probably one of the most important organs and needs to be cleansed before diseases are able to be reversed. But, if you only cleanse the colon, all of the other organs will still be toxic, which leaves the body diseased.

Through Dr. Sebi's intra-cellular detoxifying cleanse, every cell within the body will be purified. The body is then able to rejuvenate and rebuild itself.

Dr. Sebi's Diet

The Dr. Sebi diet is a plant-based alkaline diet. It helps to rejuvenate the cells in your body by getting rid of the toxic waste. The bulk of the diet is made up of a shortlist of foods along with supplements.

Dr. Sebi's diet is also able to help conditions like lupus, AIDS, kidney disease, and other diseases. The treatments for these diseases require you to eat only certain grains, fruits, and veggies, and strictly abstaining from animal products.

This is a very low protein diet, and that's what makes Dr. Sebi's supplements so important. You cannot have soy or animal products, lentils, or beans. You have several different options when it comes to Dr. Sebi's supplement choices, and you can even purchase and "all-inclusive" package that has 20 different products and can help to restore your body's health.

If you don't want to do the "all-inclusive" package, you can pick supplements according to the health problems you are suffering from. For example, Bio Ferro can help to increase overall wellbeing, help digestive issues, promote weight loss, boost immunity, cleanse the blood, and treat liver problems.

Weight Loss

While Dr. Sebi's diet isn't meant to be a weight loss diet, it can help you to lose weight. Since you will be cutting out all of the processed foods that most Western diets are made of, as well as fats, sugar, salt, and calories, you will likely lose weight.

Dr. Sebi's diet is a plant-based, vegan diet, and people who follow a plant-based diet often have a lower rate of heart disease and obesity. Plus, most of the foods you are allowed to eat are low in calories, except for oils, avocados, seeds, and nut, so even if you were to eat a lot of these foods, it is very unlikely that you are going to gain weight.

Benefits

Since you will be consuming a large number of fruits and veggies, it provides your body with many health benefits. Diets that are rich in fruits and veggies have been connected to less oxidative stress and reduced inflammation and can help to protect you from many different diseases.

Dr. Sebi's diet will also have you eating healthy fats and fiber-rich whole grains. All of these foods are connected to a lower risk of heart disease. Plus, you will be limiting those horrible processed foods, which is connected to better overall diet quality.

The biggest issue, though, that people have with Dr. Sebi's diet is that it is very restrictive and cuts out entire food groups that most people are used to eating. Plus, it can get very restrictive on the types of fruit and vegetables you are allowed to eat. Some people may struggle with this, but with some guidance and planning, you can make the switch.

CHAPTER 2

HEALING AND RECOVERING FROM STDS

STDs, which stands for sexually transmitted diseases, are still fairly prevalent even though there are well-known ways to prevent them. There are several diseases that fall into the category of STDs and are spread by sexual intercourse, but can be spread through other manners. The most common STDs are trichomoniasis, syphilis, some types of hepatitis, gonorrhea, genital warts, genital herpes, Chlamydia, and HIV.

At one time, STDs were referred to as venereal diseases. They are some of the most common contagious infections. About 65 million Americans have been diagnosed with an incurable STD. Every year, 20 million new cases occur, and about half of these are in people aged 15 to 24. All of these can have long-term implications.

These are serious illnesses that need to be treated. Some of them are considered incurable and can be deadly, such as HIV. Learning more about these diseases can provide you with knowledge on how to protect yourself.

STDs can be spread through oral, vaginal, and anal sex. Trichomoniasis is able to be contracted through contact with a moist or damp object, like toilet seats, wet clothing, or towels, although it is mostly spread through sexual contact. People who are at a higher risk of STDs include:

- Those who have more than one sexual partner.

- Those who trade sex for drugs or money.

- Those who share needles for drug use.

- Those who don't use condoms during sex.

- Those who have sex with a person who has had several partners.

Herpes and HIV are the two STDs that are chronic conditions that modern medicine can cure, but can only manage. Hepatitis B can sometimes become chronic. Unfortunately, you sometimes don't find out that you have an STD until it has damaged your reproductive organs, heart, vision, or other organs. STDs can also weaken the immune system, which leaves you vulnerable to contracting other diseases. Chlamydia and gonorrhea can cause pelvic inflammatory disease, and this can leave women unable to conceive. It is also able to kill you. If an STD is passed onto a newborn, the baby could face permanent damage, or it could kill them.

CAUSES OF STDS

In terms of modern medicine, STDs are caused by all types of infection. Syphilis, gonorrhea, and Chlamydia are bacteria. Hepatitis B, genital warts, genital herpes, and HIV are all viral. Parasites cause trichomoniasis.

The STD germs live within vaginal secretions, blood semen, and, in some cases, saliva. The majority of the organisms will be spread through oral, anal, or vaginal sex, but some, like with genital warts and genital herpes, can be spread simply through skin-to-skin contact. Hepatitis B is able to be spread through sharing personal items, like razors or toothbrushes.

PREVENTION

The most obvious step in healing for STDs is to not get one in the first place. The first tip people give in preventing STDs is to not have sex, or at least avoid sex with people who have genital discharge, rash, sores, or other symptoms. The only time you should have unprotected sex is if you and your partner are only having sex with one another, and you have both tests negative for STDs in the last six months. Otherwise, you need to make sure you:

- Use condoms whenever you have sex. If you need a lubricant, make sure that it is one that is water-based. Condoms should be used for the entire act of sex. Keep in mind; condoms aren't 100% effective when it comes to preventing pregnancy or disease. However, they are very effective if you use them the right way.

- Avoid sharing underclothing or towels.

- Bathe after and before you have sex.

- If you are okay with vaccination, you can get vaccines for a lot of STDs, specifically Hep B and HPV.

- Make sure you are tested for HIV.

- If you abuse alcohol or drugs, please seek help. It is more common for people who are under the influence to have unsafe sex.

- Lastly, abstaining from sex completely is the only 100% effective way to prevent STDs.

There was a time when it was believed that using a condom with nonoxynol-9 would prevent STDs by killing the organisms that caused them. There has been new research that has found that this can end up irritating the woman's cervix and vagina and could increase her risk of an STD. It is recommended that you avoid condoms with nonoxynol-9.

HERPES

The herpes simplex virus causes herpes infection. This affects the external genitalia, mucosal surfaces, anal region, and skin in other areas of your body. Herpes is considered to be a life-long condition. However, there are people who don't experience any symptoms even though they carry the virus.

The most common symptoms of herpes are vaginal discharge, cold sores, pain during urination, ulcers, and blisters. There is modern medicine that can help with herpes, but none of them can cure it.

There are two forms of the HSV virus: simplex one and two. Simplex one is considered oral herpes, and simplex two is genital herpes. Over 50% of the people in the US have simplex one. In the US, about 15.5% of people aged 14 to 49 have simplex two.

If you receive oral sex from a person who has a current outbreak of cold sores around the mount ups your risk of being infected. You cannot contract genital herpes from a toilet seat.

The majority of people who have been infected with herpes won't experience any symptoms for months or years. Those who do end up having an outbreak during this initial period will have it within four days of exposure, but it can range from two to 12 days.

Most people who are infected with HSV will have recurring outbreaks. When a person has first been infected with herpes, they will have recurrences more frequently. With time, though, the remission phases will get longer, and recurrences won't be as severe.

The primary infection is the outbreak of genital herpes that happens after a person has just been infected. The symptoms of the first outbreak tend to be very severe and could involve:

- Red blisters on the skin

- Cold sores on or around the mouth

- Malaise

- High temperature

- Pain during urination

- Enlarged, tender lymph nodes

- Itching and pain

- Vaginal discharge

- Ulceration and blisters on the external genitalia, on the cervix, or in the vagina

Most of the time, those sores will heal up, and there won't be any noticeable scarring. In outbreaks after the primary outbreak, the symptoms aren't as severe and don't last as long. Most of the time, symptoms don't last longer than ten days and will often include:

- Red blisters

- Cold sores on or around the mouth

- Women could have ulcers or blisters on the cervix

- Tingling or burning around the genitals before the blisters show up

If HSV is present on the skin of a person infected with it, it can be given to another person through the moist skin in the genitals, anus, and mouth. The virus can also spread to other people through contact with other areas of the skin, including the eyes.

You cannot catch HSV by touching a towel, sink, work surface, or object that was touched by the infected person. An infection will most often occur in one of the following ways:

- Having genital contact with a person who is infected.

- Sharing sex toys.

- Having oral sex from a person with current cold sores.

- Having unprotected anal or vaginal sex.

It is most common for the virus to be passed on right before the blisters appear, while visible, and until the blisters have completely gone away. HSV is also able to be passed on to another person even if there aren't any signs of a current outbreak, but it isn't that likely.

It is possible for a baby to get herpes from its mother if she has an active outbreak at the time she gives birth.

As far as modern medicine goes, there are various treatment options, most of which are home remedies. Home remedies for herpes include:

- Painkillers, like ibuprofen or acetaminophen

- Bathing in an Epsom salt bath to help relieve symptoms

- Soaking in a sitz bath

- Using petroleum jelly on the affected skin

- Avoiding tight clothing

- Washing hands well, especially when you have touched an affected area

- Abstaining from sex until the symptoms have past

- If urinating hurts, rub some lidocaine lotion or cream to the urethra

There are some people who like to apply ice packs to the affected area.

There aren't any drugs that can get rid of herpes. Doctors will sometimes prescribe antivirals, like acyclovir, which can help prevent the virus from spreading. They can also help an outbreak to clear up quicker and can help to reduce symptom severity.

Doctors will normally only prescribe antivirals the first time a person has an outbreak. Subsequent outbreaks tend to be mild, so treatment isn't normally needed.

There is also an episodic treatment option, which is used on people who have less than six outbreaks in a single year. Whenever an outbreak occurs, a doctor will prescribe a five-day course of antivirals.

If a person has more than six outbreaks in a single year, a doctor may prescribe a suppressive treatment. There are some cases where a doctor could recommend that a person takes an antiviral each day for the rest of your life. The point of this is to try and prevent anymore outbreaks. While this suppressive treatment is able to significantly reduce your risk of passing herpes onto your partner, there is still a small chance that you can.

To prevent herpes, you should follow the same prevent rules that were listed above, plus avoid kissing anybody if they have a cold sore. For most people, there are types of triggers that will cause an outbreak. These triggers could be sunbathing, friction against the skin, illness, being tired, and stress. Figuring out triggers can help to lower a person's chance of an outbreak.

Now, you can do the above, or you can try Dr. Sebi's cure. The goal of following Dr. Sebi's treatment is to create an environment where herpes can't live. Cells need to receive oxygen. Then chemicals in regular medications for herpes remove oxygen from and cells, and, most of the time, will also introduce herpes. It will take some time to help cleanse your body of herpes, but you'll do it with iron-rich plant-based items. You should start out by taking Bio Ferro and Iron Plus. Then you will need to start eating foods high in iron, which include:

- Yellow dock
- Blue vervain
- Burdock
- Lams quarters
- Dandelion
- Kale
- Purslane
- Conconsa
- Guaco
- Sarsil berry

- Sarsaparilla

Then you will want to have some bromide plus powder. The iron you are consuming is boosting your immune system, but you need to get mineral nutrition, and that's where the bromide plus powder comes in. All you have to do for this is to mix a teaspoon into a cup of boiling water. You should consume this at least two times a day.

More important than what you should consume is what you shouldn't consume. It is important that you avoid sweets and starches. You can have small amounts of sweet plant food or fruits. It is best to choose bitter foods rather than sweet. When it comes to herpes, you will want to stay away from quinoa, avocados, and chickpeas, and try to consume cactus plants, mushrooms, squash, and zucchini, as well as sea vegetables.

You can make teas out of plants like yellow dock, dandelion, and burdock. These should be consumed several times throughout the day for at least ten days. Depending on where you live, you may have to order these herbs online. You should also practice fasting. The more you are able to faster, the quicker your body will heal from herpes. If, while fasting, you start to feel weak, you can eat some dates. They may be sweet, but they won't affect your cells. Make sure you only eat them if you feel weak.

You should also eat plenty of salads. As a rule of thumb, eat salad as if you were eating a bag of potato chips, but don't eat iceberg.

HIV

HIV has been, and for many, still is one of the scariest STDs you can contract. HIV stands for human immunodeficiency virus and can lead to AIDS, acquired immunodeficiency syndrome. There are a lot of "beliefs" about HIV/AIDS, most of which are unfounded and are caused by ill-informed gossip.

HIV harms the immune system by killing the white blood cells that you need to fight off infections. This places a person at risk for developing some serious infections and certain types of cancers. Once HIV reaches its final stages, it becomes AIDS, but not everybody who contracts HIV will develop AIDS. For a long time, people thought HIV and AIDS were one and the same, but they aren't.

The most common way for HIV to be spread is through unprotected sex with an HIV positive person. It can also be spread through shared drug needles or contact with the blood of an infected person. Women are also able to give it to their children during childbirth or pregnancy.

Some of the first signs of an HIV infection could be flu-like symptoms and swollen glands. These could also come and go within a couple of weeks to a month. You may not experience severe symptoms until several months or years later. You could experience a primary infection or acute HIV. Most of those who have been infected will develop flu-like symptoms within a couple of months after exposure. This is what is known as the primary infection. Some of the most common signs of the primary infection are:

- Swollen lymph glands, mostly in the neck

- Painful mouth sores and sore throat

- Rash

- Joint pain and muscle aches

- Headache

- Fever

It is possible that these symptoms could be so mild that they may go unnoticed. However, how much of the virus you have in your bloodstream is very high during this stage. This is why the infection will spread more easily during this time than once you reach the next stage.

The next stage is the clinical latent infection or chronic HIV. For some, they will still have swollen lymph nodes. Otherwise, there aren't any really specific symptoms and signs. HIV will say in the body and your white blood cells. If one does not get diagnosed and receive some sort of therapy, this stage can last for ten years. Some people will develop severe secondary diseases a lot sooner.

Then there is the symptomatic HIV infection. As the virus starts to grow and kill off your immune cells, you could start to develop chronic signs or mild infections, like:

- Shingles

- Oral yeast infections

- Weight loss

- Diarrhea

- Swollen lymph nodes

- Fatigue

- Fever

With better antiviral medicines, most HIV patients don't develop AIDS. If left untreated, HIV will normally turn into AIDS within 10 years. Once AIDS develops, the immune system has already been severely damaged. It places a person at a higher risk of opportunistic cancers or infections, which are a disease that a person with a healthy immune system wouldn't have to worry about. The most common signs and symptoms of these secondary infections could include:

- Skin bumps or rashes

- Weight loss

- Persistent and unexplained fatigue

- Persistent white spots or odd lesions in your mouth or on the tongue

- Chronic diarrhea

- Recurring fever

- Soaking night sweats

HIV can only be spread through sex or contact with blood, or from mother to child during childbirth, pregnancy, or breastfeeding. When it comes to contact with blood, the blood has to entire a mucous membrane, such as the nose, mouth, anus, or vagina. Simply touching infected blood won't spread HIV, and once the blood is dried, it isn't dangerous.

The most common ways for HIV to be spread is:

- Sex – This is one of the most common ways for it to be spread. You can get infected by having unprotected oral, anal, or vaginal sex with an infected person whose vaginal secretions, semen, or blood enters your body. The virus is able to enter into the body through mouth sores, or through small tears that can occur in the vagina or rectum during sex.

- Blood Transfusions – At one time, people could end up contracting HIV through a blood transfusion. Nowadays, American blood banks and hospitals screen the blood for HIV antibodies, so the odds of this happening now are small.

- Sharing Needles – The second most common way for HIV to be spread is by sharing contaminated intravenous drug paraphernalia. This also puts you at a higher risk of contracting other infectious diseases, like hepatitis.

- Breastfeeding, Pregnancy, or Delivery – Mothers who are HIV-positive can pass it onto their babies. Mothers who make sure that they are receiving treatment are able to lower the risk of passing it along.

Some rumors and lies were spread during the HIV epidemic in the '80s, and unfortunately, some of those have persisted. All of these beliefs can be dispelled through simple research and common sense. The most common misconception is how it is spread. Many people are afraid to touch an HIV-positive person because they think they can contract it that way, but you can't. HIV cannot be contracted through ordinary contact. This means that you are not able to get it by shaking hands, dancing, kissing, or hugging somebody that is infected. It also cannot be spread through insect bites, water, or air. It is actually very hard to catch.

HIV also doesn't care about your color or sexual orientation. While the bulk of the infections in the US back in the '80s seemed to affect men who had sexual intercourse with other men, it is now clear that it can be spread through heterosexual sexual intercourse as well. People of any sexual orientation, sex, race, or age can become infected. However, you place yourself at a greater risk if you:

- Have unprotected sex. If you use a polyurethane or latex condoms whenever you have sex, you will greatly reduce your risk of contracting HIV. Anal sex tends to be riskier. Your risk also increases if you have multiple sexual partners.

- Use intravenous drugs. A lot of intravenous drug users will share syringes and needles. This will expose you to droplets of blood from other people.

- Have an STD. A lot of STDs will cause open sores on your genitals. These sores provide HIV access to your body.

- Are uncircumcised. There are studies that have found that a lack of circumcision can increase the risk of HIV transmission.

Since HIV weakens your immune system, it can put you at a higher risk of developing several different infections and some forms of cancers.

- Tuberculosis – For nations who are resource-limited, TB is often the most common opportunistic infection. It is also the leading cause of death for people with AIDS.

- Candidiasis – This is a common HIV-related infection. This will create inflammation as well as a thick, white coating over the mucous membranes of the vagina, esophagus, tongue, or mouth.

- Cytomegalovirus – This herpes virus is spread through body fluids like breast milk, semen, urine, blood, and saliva. The body of a person with a healthy immune system will inactivate the virus, and it stays dormant inside of the body. With a weakened immune system, this virus will resurface, which can damage the lungs, digestive tract, eyes, and other organs.

- Cryptococcal Meningitis – Meningitis occurs when the membranes and fluid around the spinal cord and brain become inflamed. This is a very common central nervous system infection connected to HIV and is caused by a fungus.

- Cryptosporidiosis – This infection occurs from an intestinal parasite that is common in animals. It is contracted when a person eats or drinks contaminated water or food. The parasite will then grow within the bile ducts and intestines and will lead to chronic and severe diarrhea for those with AIDS.

- Toxoplasmosis – Toxoplasma gondii causes this potentially deadly infection. It is a parasite, which is mainly spread by cats. The infected cats will pass the parasite along in their feces, which can end up spreading to humans and other animals. Seizures will occur if this spreads to the brain.

- Lymphoma – This is a cancer that begins in the white blood cells. Painless swelling of the lymph nodes in the groin, armpit, or neck is the most common early signs.

- Kaposi's Sarcoma – This is a tumor that forms in the blood vessel walls, and is very rare in those who do not have HIV. It appears as purple, red, or pink lesions on the mouth and skin. People who have a darker skin tone, the lesions could look black or dark brown. It can also affect the internal organs.

- Kidney Disease – HIVAN is an inflammation of the filters in the kidneys that can get rid of excess wastes and fluid. This most often affects Hispanics or African Americans.

- Neurological Complications – While AIDS doesn't actually infect the nerve cells; it can end up causing neurological symptoms like difficulty walking, anxiety, depression, forgetfulness, and confusion. The most common neurological problem is the AIDS dementia complex, which can end up causing reduced mental functioning and behavioral changes.

- Wasting Syndrome –This happens when a person loses at least ten percent of their body weight and is accompanied by fever, chronic weakness, and diarrhea. This is not as common anymore.

A blood test is needed to find out if there is an HIV infection. There are home testing kits, or you can go to your regular doctor. There are also some free testing sites that you can find by calling the CDC hotline, 1-800-CDC-INFO. These tests look for antibodies to the virus. Unfortunately, it can take up to 12 weeks for the body to develop these antibodies. There is a quick test that looks for HIV antigens, which is a protein that is produced by HIV right after you have been infected. This gives you the chance to be diagnosed sooner so that you can take swift steps to prevent spreading the virus.

Once a person has been diagnosed with the disease, there are a lot of tests that your doctor can perform to figure out what stage the disease is in and the best treatment methods. These include:

- Drug Resistance – There are some strains of HIV that are resistant to medications. This test will help the doctor to figure out if your strain of the virus is resistant and will help to guide them as to the best treatment options.

- HIV RNA Viral Load –This test looks at how much of the virus is in your blood. Having a higher viral load has been connected to a worse outcome.

- CD4 T Cell Count – T cells are the white blood cells that HIV targets and destroys. Even if you are not experiencing any symptoms, HIV turns into AIDS once your T cells drop below 200.

Doctors will sometimes order lab tests that check for complications and secondary infections, which could include:

- Urinary tract infection

- Kidney or liver damage

- Sexually transmitted infections

- Toxoplasmosis

- Hepatitis

- Tuberculosis

Modern medicine has yet to find a cure for HIV, but there are a lot of medications that can help to fight the HIV infection and lower a person's risk of infecting other people. People who are able to get treated early are able to live a long life with the disease, which has not always been the case.

Treatments for HIV are called antiretroviral therapy or ART. The various classes of drugs work by blocking the virus in various ways. ART is a recommended treatment for everybody, no matter what their T cell levels are. They recommend that a patient is given three drugs that come from two different classes so that a drug-resistant strain of HIV isn't created. The different classes of drugs are:

- Integrase Inhibitors – These work by disabling integrase, a protein, which HIV often usesto add its genetic material into T cells. Some common drugs in this class are Tivicay and Isentress.

- Fusion or Entry Inhibitors – These drugs work by blocking HIV's entry into T cells. Common drugs are Selzentry and Fuzeon.

- Protease Inhibitors – These drugs work by inactivating HIV protease, which is another protein that HIV uses to copy itself. Some common drugs of this class are Crixivan, Lexiva, Prezista, and Reyataz.

- Nucleotide or Nucleoside Reverse Transcriptase Inhibitors – These drugs introduce faulty versions of the building tools that HIV has to use to copy itself. Ziagen is one example, and then you have the combination drugs Combivir, Descovy, and Truvada.

- Non-Nucleoside Reverse Transcriptase Inhibitors – These drugs shut off the protein that HIV needs to copy itself. Some common drugs are Viramune, Intelence, and Sustiva.

Most HIV treatments will require you to take several different pills at certain times during the day for the remainder of your life. Every medication will come with its own side effects that you will have to get used to. It is very important that you go to regular check-ups with your doctor to keep an eye on your health and your treatment progress. Some of the most common side effects of treatment include:

- High blood sugar levels

- Abnormal cholesterol levels

- Breakdown of muscle tissue

- Bone loss or weakened bones

- Heart disease

- Diarrhea, nausea, or vomiting

As you age, there are some age-related health issues that can become more difficult to manage. There are medications that you might have been given otherwise, for age-related diseases, that don't interact very well with your HIV medications. This will involve speaking with your doctor and monitoring every situation.

Once you are on a treatment plan, your doctor will constantly monitor your T cells and viral load to determine how you are responding to your treatment. T cells need to be checked every three to six months. The viral load needs to be tested every three to four months. The goal of the treatment is to lower your viral load so that it is not able to be detected. This in no way means that your HIV has been treated. It simply means that your levels are too low for the test to detect them.

Besides medical treatments, a person will also be advised to make certain lifestyle changes to help.

- Take off Your Pets – There are some animals that carry parasites that can end up causing infections in those who have HIV. Cat feces can end up causing toxoplasmosis. Salmonella is found in reptiles. Birds can also pass along histoplasmosis or cryptococcus. It is important that you wash your hands extremely well after you have handled your pets or cleaned their litter box.

- Make Sure You Get Immunizations – It is often suggested that HIV-positive individuals receive regular flu and pneumonia vaccinations to prevent secondary diseases. It is also important that the vaccines are not live viruses because these can be very dangerous for those with weakened immune systems.

- Stay Away from Raw Eggs, Meat, and More – Foodborne illnesses are more dangerous for people who have HIV. HIV-positive individuals should never eat anything that is raw or unpasteurized.

- Eat Healthy Foods – Fresh veggies and fruits, as well as whole grains, can help to keep and HIV-positive individuals strong and healthy and can help support the immune system.

The treatment goes beyond the actual treatment of the disease. It also involved coping and support. Getting a diagnosis like HIV is devastating. The financial, emotional, and social consequences of HIV can make it a lot harder to cope with the illness, and this is true for those closest to you as well.

There are a lot of resources and services that can help HIV-positive people. Most clinics will have nurses, social workers, or counselors who are able to help you directly or direct you to someone who is able to. Some services could include:

- Giving your support when you are in a financial emergency

- Help you with legal and employment issues

- Help with child care and housing

- Arrange transportation to and from doctors appointments

The same strategies to prevent any other STD are the same strategies that you should use to decrease your risk of contracting HIV. There are some medications that people can take that can keep them from contracting HIV, but these are normally only given to patients who are at a higher risk of contracting it.

Dr. Sebi offers an alternative to modern medicine when it comes to treating HIV. He believes that cleaning the mucus buildup in the lymphatic system and blood can help HIV.

Dr. Sebi didn't create something specifically to treat HIV/AIDS or any specific disease. Instead, he came up with compounds that are meant to cleanse the body and provide important nutrition. However, when you want to focus on cleansing your body of major illnesses, the interest will then turn to compounds that are found in his therapeutic packages.

We are all dealing with the fatigue and cellular stress because we are constantly exhausting out oxygen supply. And we are constantly trying to find any means to remain hydrated to deal with our suffocation through animal products, medical-chemicals, starch, and sugar.

We need out mucous membrane to maintain health because it helps to protect the cells. If this mucus is broken down, it becomes pus and will then expose your cells, which is what causes disease.

Now, when we are fasting, it will cause our bodies to form more oxygen. Then we start to provide our bodies with foods that are rich in potassium phosphate and iron fluorine, which helps to flush out toxins, tumors, and mucus from our internal walls.

The reason we need to cleanse ourselves is that we know that our liver, intestines, and pancreas are power players for the best circulation. This will help to treat HIV/AIDS.

The only thing that is going to cause your body to start harming your mucous membranes is acid. This erosion in the body will create a greater oxygen deprivation. It is important that when you eat, you consume natural greens and fruits. Any grains you eat should not be man-made, and that all oils you use can retain nutrition once it is processed. Springwater will also help you to maintain your mineral content.

Dr. Sebi has come up with more than 40 herbs to flush your body of inflammation as well as nourish it. While many people will travel to Usha Village in Honduras to be cured of HIV/AIDs, you don't have to travel that far. All you need to do is stick to the nutritional guide and make sure you consume only alkaline foods.

The lymphatic system, skin, and blood make up the immunological system. It is important that you adhere to a strict diet to clear these areas of mucus. If you don't, it will take a lot longer to heal. To help boost your healing, you should consume only green leafy plants such as:

- Nori

- Hijiki

- Arame

- Dulce

- Wakame

- Burdock plants

- Lams quarters

- Purslane

- Nopales

- Dandelion greens

- Lettuce

You can also eat mushrooms, spices, and peppers that are on the approved foods list. When you start to follow this diet, it is important that you make sure you drink a gallon of water every day and do some light exercise. Having a gallon jug prepared for the day, at the start of the day, is a good idea, and you can count any water used in teas. You should drink red clover tea instead of chamomile.

The first thing you need to do is to address your iron deficiency because your immune system requires plenty of it. You need to take a bottle a day of either Bio Ferro or Iron Plus for ten days. After that, you only have to take two to three spoonfuls once you begin your therapeutic package. You can also consume a cup of bromide tea at noon and in the evening each day.

After that, the initial first ten days, you should start taking a mixture of different supplements. Some people will take all of them, while others only choose a select few. There are people on Dr. Sebi's website that can help guide you as to what you need to take. The following products are the ones you should look at:

- Electra Cell – breaks down calcification and strengthens your immune system, and clears out the buildup of mucus.

- Cell Cleanser – Gets rid of mucus, acids, and toxins on the intracellular level, and will improve your bowel movements.

- CC4 – Gets rid of mucus, acids, and toxins on a deeper intracellular level and will help provide you with mineral nourishment.

- Chelation – Helps to cleanse you on an intracellular level, and improves your bowel movements. It also helps your digestive tract.

- DBT –Helps to nourish and cleanse your pancreas.

- ECAL – Removes fluid and toxins from your cells' mitochondria. It is high in carbonates, phosphates, bromides, and iodides.

- Fucus – This is a natural diuretic. It will flush out stagnant fluids, dead cells, and promotes healthy skin. It contains phosphates, calcium, magnesium, and other important minerals.

- Lino – Get rids of calcification in the body. It has a lot of important minerals, which is important for the body and helps to break up and dissolve calcification.

- Lupulo – Calms the nervous system, relieves pain, and breaks up inflammation.

If you follow Dr. Sebi's diet and start taking his supplements, you can improve HIV/AIDs. That being said, it is still a good idea to continue to go to your doctor for monitoring. It is okay to take medications that your doctor prescribes while doing this. As you will read in the nutritional guide, the important thing is to take your supplements an hour before you take medications. This allows the supplements to help your body and heal your body from any ill-effects the medications could cause.

Lastly, you may have noticed that Dr. Sebi's treatments for herpes and HIV are very similar. While there are slight differences, most treatments will follow along the same lines as these. That means if you start following the treatment for one disease, you will be helping to prevent other diseases.

CHAPTER 3

DR. SEBI'S SECRET TO REVERSING DIABETES

Diabetes occurs when your blood glucose becomes too high. Blood glucose is what your body uses as energy, and is created from whatever you eat. Insulin, which is a hormone that your pancreas makes, helps the glucose move into your cells so that it can be used as energy. There are times when the body doesn't make enough, or any, insulin. Then there are times when the body doesn't use the insulin correctly. This causes the glucose to remain in your blood, and it won't reach your cells.

The longer that this goes on, the excess glucose in the blood can end up creating severe health problems. Luckily, there is a way to reverse diabetes, and modern medicine also has medicine that can help manage diabetes if a person chooses not to make drastic dietary changes.

People can also be diagnosed with pre-diabetes. At this stage, it is easier to reverse things and prevent diabetes from developing at all. But that does not mean pre-diabetes is any less important than full-blown diabetes.

While type 1 and type 2 diabetes have different causes, there are still two factors that work in both. A person inherits some predisposition to this particular disease, and then something in your environment triggers the onset. Genes by themselvesare not enough. A good example of this is with identical twins. For identical twins, they have identical genes, but when one of them develops type 1 diabetes, the other one will only develop the disease, at most, half the time. If one of the develops type 2 diabetes, the odds of the other one developing it to is three in four.

Types of Diabetes

There isn't just one type of diabetes that a person can be diagnosed with. There are actually several different types. The most common forms are type 1, type 2, and gestational.

Type 1 diabetes is something that can't be avoided and is normally found in childhood, and is often referred to as juvenile diabetes. It is a type of auto-immune disease. In this case, your body doesn't make enough insulin. The immune system will also attack and destroy the pancreatic cells that create insulin. Most people with type 1 diabetes will have to take insulin every single day.

About five percent of people with diabetes have type 1 diabetes. Type 1 diabetes is considered incurable, but there are a lot of management tools out there. Some of the most common symptoms of type 1 diabetes are:

- Weight loss without an apparent reason

- Fatigue and tiredness

- Unclear or blurred vision and problems with sight

- Frequent urination

- Increased thirst and hunger

Once a person is diagnosed with type 1 diabetes, they enter the honeymoon phase. During this time, the cells that are responsible for secreting insulin could continue to make the hormone for a bit before stopping altogether. At this stage, they won't need as many insulin shots to keep their glucose levels.

This often causes the sufferer to think they are getting better. Even if things seem good, they need to make sure they are still closely monitoring their numbers. People with type 1 diabetes that go unmanaged can face dangerous complications. This can include:

- Diabetic retinopathy - Too much glucose can weaken the walls in the retina, which is the part of the eye that detects color and light. As this continues to progress, small blood vessels behind the eye could bulge and rupture, creating vision problems.

- Diabetic neuropathy - Too much glucose can reduce your circulation and damage the nerves in the feet and hands, which can cause pain, tingling, and burning sensations.

- Kidney disease - Since the kidneys filter glucose out of the blood, having to do this too much can cause kidney failure.

Some other issues people could face are depression, gum disease, and cardiovascular disease. Diabetic ketoacidosis is a complication that happens when the body is not given the right amount of insulin, and it places the body under great stress. This causes very high levels of blood sugar. At this point, the body has started to break down fat and not sugar and produces ketones. These ketones can become harmful if too many are produced, which causes acidosis. This is a medical emergency, and it will require hospitalization.

People with type 1 diabetes are faced with having to take insulin for the rest of their life. You will work with your doctor to figure out the best schedule for your insulin doses. There are now continuous blood sugar monitors and insulin pumps. This hybrid machine can act as an artificial pancreas and remove the need for remembering when to take insulin. They will still need to manually check their blood sugar levels to make sure things are still okay.

Most of the time, for a person to develop type 1 diabetes, people are going to have to inherit a risk factor from both of their parents. It is believed that these factors tend to be higher in Caucasians because there is a higher rate of type 1 diabetes among Caucasians.

Since most people at risk for this don't develop diabetes, researchers want to figure out the environmental triggers. One trigger could be cold weather. Type 1 diabetes tends to show up more often during the winter months than summer and tends to be more prevalent in colder climates. They also believe that viruses could be another trigger. It is possible that a virus that has little to no effect on most can end up triggering type 1 diabetes in others.

Diet as an infant may also play a role. Type 1 diabetes isn't as common in those who breastfed and in those who started eating solid foods at a later age. For most people, developing type 1 diabetes tends to take several years.

A man with type 1 diabetes has a 1 in 17 chance of having a child who develops it as well. A woman with type 2 diabetes, and gives birth before the age of 25, there is a 1 in 25 risk that your child will develop it. If you give birth after the age of 25, the odds go down to 1 in 100.

A child's risk becomes doubled if you ended up developing diabetes before you were 11. If you and your partner have type 1 diabetes, the risk becomes 1 in 10 and 1 in 4. There are tests that can be given to find out your child's risk of developing type 1 diabetes.

Type 2 diabetes is acquired during life because of poor dietary choices, and sometimes genetics. It is most often caused by depleting your insulin resources to the point when the body is not able to make or use insulin correctly. This can be developed at any age, and even as a child. However, it is more common for middle-aged and older adults to be diagnosed. This is the most common form of diabetes. There are many risk factors for developing type 2 diabetes. They can include:

- Leading a sedentary life

- Being older than 45

- Being of Asian-Pacific Islander, Latin American, Native American, or African American descent

- A history of PCOS

- Give birth to a child that weighed more than nine pounds, or having gestational diabetes

- History of high blood pressure

- Having an HDL cholesterol level that is less than 40 or 50 mg/dL

- Family history of diabetes

- Being overweight

The family lineage factor for type 2 diabetes is a lot stronger than it is for type 1 diabetes. Studies in twins have found that genetics plays a very big role in developing type 2. Yet, the environment still plays a big role as well. Lifestyle tends to play a very big role as well. Obesity often runs in families, and families will often have similar exercise and eating habits.

Gestational diabetes only affects women during pregnancy. For the most part, diabetes will go away once the woman gives birth, but it puts the baby at a higher risk of developing diabetes. The mother is also at a higher risk of developing type 2 diabetes later in life.

There are also less common types of diabetes, such as monogenic diabetes that is inherited, and diabetes-related to cystic fibrosis.

As mentioned earlier, people can be diagnosed with pre-diabetes. Doctors diagnose people with pre-diabetes when blood sugar reaches a range of 100 to 125 mg/dL. Normal blood sugar levels are normally 70 to 99 mg/dL. A person who has diabetes will have a blood sugar high than 126 mg/dL when fasted.

Pre-diabetes simply means that you have a blood sugar level that is higher than it should be but isn't high enough to be considered diabetes. It does place you at a greater risk of developing type 2 diabetes. If a doctor finds that a person has pre-diabetes, they will suggest that the person start making healthy life changes to stop the progression. Eating healthier foods and losing weight will often prevent the development of diabetes.

A1C

Anybody with diabetes is going to hear the term A1C. This is a type of blood test that only those with type 2 diabetes and pre-diabetes will have to take. This test will measure the average blood sugar levels for the last the three months. Doctors can use an A1C test on their own, or they can use it in combination with other tests for diabetes in order to make an accurate diagnosis. They will also use A1C tests to see well you are taking care of yourself and managing your diabetes. This is very different than a simple blood sugar check that diabetics will give themselves every day.

The results of an A1C test are shown in percentages. The higher a percentage, the higher your blood sugar has been. The various levels include:

- Normal A1C levels are below 5.7%.

- Pre-diabetes tends to be between 5.7 and 6.4 percent. Those with these levels will likely have their A1Cs retested every year.

- Type 2 diabetes is when you have an A1C of 6.5% or higher.

- For people who have diabetes, they need to take an A1C test at least two times a year. The goal for diabetics is to have an A1C below a seven.

The Purpose of Insulin

The hormones in your body are chemical messengers that tell certain tissues or cells to act in a specific way that supports different functions of your body. Insulin is an important hormone to help you live.

The pancreas is located behind the stomach and is the main source of insulin. There are clusters of cells in the pancreas that are called islets, and they produce insulin, and they also determine how much needs to be produces based on the amount of the blood glucose levels.

The more glucose that is present in the body, the more insulin will have to be produced in order to balance out the sugar levels. Insulin also helps to break down proteins and fats.

There is a delicate balance of insulin that regulates blood sugar and several other processes within the body. If the insulin levels end up becoming too high or low, these excessive levels can start to create certain symptoms. If this state of high or low blood sugar were to continue, a person could end up developing some serious health problems.

For some people, their immune system will start to attack these islets, and then they will stop producing insulin, or at least not produce enough. This is what causes type 1 diabetes.

For some people, especially ones who are inactive, obese, or overweight, insulin will no longer be effective in transporting glucose to the cells and isn't able to fulfill all of the actions it needs to. When insulin is unable to exert its effect where it needs to, it creates insulin resistance.

Type 2 diabetes will be developed once the islets can't produce the right about of insulin to overcome this insulin resistance. Since around the early 1900s, doctors could isolate insulin and give it to people in an injectable form to help them supplement the hormone.

What Causes Problems with Insulin?

Doctors have yet to figure out what causes type 1 diabetes. Type 2 diabetes, on the other hand, has much clearer causes. Insulin gives glucose access to the cells to supply them with energy. Insulin resistance normally occurs once the following cycle has happened:

1. An individual has an environment or genes that make it more likely that they won't be able to make enough insulin to handle the amount of glucose they consume.

2. The body starts to try and make enough insulin to process all of the blood glucose.

3. The pancreas is unable to keep up with the extra demand, and then excess blood sugar will start to circulate throughout the blood, creating damage.

4. With time, insulin won't be as effective at moving glucose into the cells, and blood sugar will continue to increase.

This insulin resistance will happen at a gradual pace. This is the reason why doctors say that you should make lifestyle changes in order to reverse or slowdown the cycle.

Hyperinsulinemia

Hyperinsulinemia refers to having higher amounts of insulin in your blood than what is seen as normal. This does not mean that a person has diabetes, but this is closely connected to type 2 diabetes.

Hyperinsulinemia tends to be caused by insulin resistance. The body continues to try and compensate for this problem by making more insulin. This can end up causing type 2 diabetes. In rare cases, hyperinsulinemia is caused by:

- Too much or growth of insulin-producing cells within your pancreas

- A rare tumor of the insulin-producing cells

There are normally no signs or symptoms for hyperinsulinemia, except when people who have a tumor, and it ends up causing low blood sugar.

Taking Insulin and Medications

Those who have type 1 diabetes, and some with type 2, will have to inhale or inject insulin to help regulate their blood sugar levels. There are a lot of different types of insulin that you may be prescribed. Most of them are grouped by the length of time that their effects last. These groups include long-acting, intermediate, regular, and rapid.

There are some who take long-acting insulin to help maintain a consistent low blood sugar level. Others will choose short-acting insulin, or use a combination. Whatever a person chooses, they will typically check their glucose levels with a fingerstick.

Checking blood sugar levels in this manner will involve using a machine that is known as a glucometer. Those with type 1 diabetes will use this reading to help them figure out the amount of insulin they should take. Self-monitoring is the best and only way to keep track of your blood sugar levels. Assuming what your glucose levels are based on how you feel can be dangerous unless you think you have extremely low glucose.

Insulin tends to be what allows diabetics to live an active life. However, it can often cause side effects, especially if you take too much. Too much insulin can end up causing hypoglycemia, or very low blood sugar, and this can cause shaking, nausea, and sweating.

This is why people have to be taught to measure their insulin correctly and to make sure that they consume a balanced diet. Besides taking insulin, there are other types of medications that diabetics may be prescribed.

For type 2 diabetes, the doctor may prescribe Metformin. This can come in liquid or pill form. This works by lowering blood sugar and makes insulin more effective. This pill isn't meant to help you lose weight, so it is important to change your diet. Besides diabetes, a person could also have other health problems, and these should be controlled as well.

There are also GLP-1 receptor agonists and SGLT2 inhibitors. These were implemented about new guidelines that were introduced in 2018 for people who had chronic kidney disease and atherosclerotic cardiovascular disease.

GLP-1 receptor agonists help diabetics by increasing how much insulin the body is able to produce and decreases how much glucose enters the bloodstream. This drug is injectable. Some will use this along with metformin, or they will take it alone. Some of the most common side effects are loss of appetite and nausea.

SLGT2 inhibitors are a new type of drug the works by lowering glucose levels. It works separate to insulin, and they could be great for those who aren't quite ready for insulin. This can be taken by mouth. Some common side effects are a higher risk of genital and urinary infections, as well as ketoacidosis.

Self-Monitoring

Whatever path you choose for reversing and controlling your diabetes, you should still keep up with self-monitoring. This can help you to regulate your meal schedule, when medication is taking, and physical activity.

While the glucose machines can vary quite a bit, they will have three main components, the meter, lancing device, and a test strip. The lancing device will be used to prick the skin to draw a bit of blood, which is then placed on the test strip.

Each meter will come with its own instructions on how to use the device. However, the following tips will likely apply for a lot of machines out there:

- Both of your hands need to be clean and dry before you touch anything.

- You should never use a test strip more than once, and you should keep them in their original container to make sure that they aren't exposed to external moisture, which can affect the reading.

- Keep the container closed after testing.

- Make sure you keep an eye on the expiration date.

- Older meters can sometimes require coding before you use it. Make sure you check your current machine to see if it requires this.

- Keep the strips and meter in a cool, dry area.

- Always have your strips and meter with you when going to consultations. This will allow your physician to make sure they are effective.

When you are using a self-monitoring your diabetes, you will need to use a lancet to prick your skin. While the thought of drawing blood could make people a little nervous, the lancing of the finger to get the blood for your test should be a simple and gentle act. You should always follow these precautions:

- Make sure you wash the area that is to be pricked with soapy, warm water to make sure that food residue won't distort the readings.

- Make sure you use a thin, small lancet for max comfort.

- The lancet will, after having depth settings to control how deep the prick will be. Adjust this to what feels comfortable to you.

- A lot of meters will need a teardrop-sized blood sample.

- Taking blood from the side of your finger doesn't cause as much pain. The little, ring, or middle finger can be more comfortable.

- While there are some meters that will allow samples taken from other sites, like upper arms and thighs, the outer palm and fingertips produce a more accurate reading.

- Bring the blood to the surface by using a "milking" motion instead of pressing onto the lancing site.

- Get rid of the lances in accordance with local regulations for disposing of share objects.

While keeping up with self-monitoring will involve lifestyle changes, it shouldn't be uncomfortable.

How Common?

In 2015, it was said that 30.3 million people in the US had diabetes, which comes out to about 9.4% of the population. Of those, more than one in four didn't know they had the disease. One in four people over the age of 65 are affected by diabetes. 90 to 95 percent of all diabetes cases in adults are due to type 2 diabetes.

A person is more likely to develop type 2 diabetes if they are 45 or older, overweight, or have a family history of diabetes. Race, physical inactivity, and certain health issues like high blood pressure can also affect your odds ofdeveloping diabetes. Gestational diabetes and pre-diabetes also put you at a higher risk of developing type 2 diabetes.

Side Effects of Diabetes

If your high blood sugar is not regulated and controlled, it will eventually cause more serious health problems. Diabetes is considered a chronic condition. The ADA says that diabetes is the seventh leading cause of death among Americans. It is manageable and reversible, but the complications associated with it can become fatal if you don't treat them properly. This can include:

- Foot problems, which could include numbness, ulcers, and untreated cuts and injuries

- Dental and gum disease

- Nerve damage

- Dental disease

- Eye problems and loss of vision

- Kidney disease

- Stroke

- Heart disease

When it comes to kidney disease, it could end up leading to kidney failure, water retention because the body cannot dispose of water, and a person could end up experience difficult bladder control.

Lifestyle Changes for Diabetes

The first thing a doctor will tell a person with diabetes is to make some lifestyle changes to help support a healthy life and weight loss. Doctors may send you to a special nutritionist who can help you to manage the condition. Some of the most common changes diabetics are told make include:

- Recognize the signs for low blood sugar when they are exercising, which includes profuse sweating, weakness, confusion, and dizziness.

- Engage in at least 30 minutes of exercise each day, five days a week. Some of the best exercises for diabetics include swimming, biking, aerobics, and walking.

- Abstaining from drinking alcohol, or cutting back to one glass a day for women and two for men.

- Staying away from high-sugar foods that only provide you with empty calories or calories that won't provide you with any nutritional benefits, like sweets, fried foods, and sodas.

- Eating a diet that is high in nutritious and fresh foods, like whole grains, healthy fats, vegetables, and fruits.

Lowering your BMI is also a great way to manage type 2 diabetes without the need for medications. Making your weight loss slow and steady will help you to retain the benefits.

Dr. Sebi

While there is a lot of good advice for diabetics that doctors will share, such as lifestyle changes, there is also a lot of medication that you could end up being prescribed. And let's not get started on how scary it must be to learn how to give yourself insulin injections.

Dr. Sebi's diabetes cure is a super simple plan, and it doesn't cost that much. Very few people wanted to try his plan at first because it required fasting. Most would rather cut off their feet than not eat. Dr. Sebi was able to cure his diabetes with a 27 day fast.

There are a lot of other people who have reported similar results as well. You can find a lot of videos on YouTube, where people talk about having cured their diabetes with Dr. Sebi's plan.

Like with the STD treatments, the goal is to rid the body of excess mucus. For diabetics, the excess mucus is found in the pancreatic duct. Dr. Sebi's own mother started fasting to help her diabetes, and after 57 days, she was cured.

During your fast, you should drink water, and you can also have herbal tea. A great herbal tea to drink is a combination of burdock, black walnut leaf, red raspberry, and elderberry. Use a tablespoon of each and mix them into one and a half liters of spring water. Bring this to a boil and let it steep for 15 minutes. Take this off the heat and mix in another half liter of water. Strain out the herbs and place to the side to use the next day.

Store the tea in the fridge and drink as much as you want during the day.

A lot of people, when they hear the word fast, assume that means they can't take anything by mouth. But that's not Dr. Sebi's fast. See, when Dr. Sebi fasted to cure his diabetes, he would take three green plus tablets each day and drink sea moss tea, spring water, and tamarind juice. You don't have to drink tamarind juice, though. Any juice that is on the approved list of foods is okay. It must be fresh juice, though. You don't want pre-made juice with a bunch of added sugars.

Once you have fasted for a while, and your body will let you know when you have had enough, you will then need to start the Dr. Sebi approved diet plan. Along with that, you should also think about taking black seeds, mulberry leaves, and fig leaves. Research on black seeds has found that taking as little as two teaspoons of the powder each day can reverse diabetes.

Figleaves are the top alternative medicine for diabetes on the market today. Mulberry leaves are a common treatment for diabetes in the Middle East. These can be made into a tea, and you can mix in some black seeds as well.

Some other foods that you should consider adding to your diet are ginseng, okra, ginger, fenugreek, red clover, swiss chard, avocado, and bitter melon.

CHAPTER 4

HAIR LOSS DOESN'T HAVE TO BE PERMANENT

Alopecia or hair loss is a problem for children, women, and men. Treatments include hair restoration techniques, hair replacements, or medicines like Rogaine and Propecia.

There is hair everywhere on the human body except the soles of the feet and the palms of the hand. We do have some hairs that are so fine that they are hard to see. Hair is made from a protein known as keratin. This is made in the hair follicles on the outer layer of our skin. When the follicles make new hair, the old get pushed out of the skin's surface of a rate of six inches each year. The hair that is visible to the naked eye is actually a string of dead keratin cells. A normal adult head will have around 100,000 to 150,000 hairs. It will lose around 100 of these every single day. When you find some stray hair in your hairbrush isn't anything to be worried about.

Most of the time, around 90 percent of the hair on your head will be growing. Every follicle has its own individual life cycle that gets influenced by disease, age, and other factors. This cycle can be divided into three phases:

- Anagen: This phase will last about two to six years. This is when the hair is actively growing.

- Catagen: This phase will only last about two or three weeks. This is a period of transitional hair growth.

- Telogen: This phase will last around two or three months. This is a time of rest. When this phase is over, the old hair is shed, and new hair will replace it. The cycle begins all over again.

When people begin aging, their hair growth rate will slow down. There are several types of hair loss:

- Scarring Alopecias

This can result in permanent hair loss. Acne, folliculitis, and cellulitis, which are all inflammatory skin conditions among other disorders like lichen planus and lupus, can cause scars that will get rid of the hair's ability to regenerate. Hair that is woven too tightly and using hot instruments that pull on the hair can cause permanent hair loss.

- Telogen Effluvium

This is a temporary thinning of the hair that happens due to changes in the hair's growth cycle. Many hairs go into a resting phase at one time, this causes the hair to shed and then thin.

- Trichotillomania

This is mostly seen in small children. It is a psychological disorder where they pull out their own hair.

- Alopecia Universalis

This can cause all the hair on the body to fall out, including pubic hair, eyelashes, and eyebrows.

- Alopecia Areata

This usually begins all of a sudden and can cause some patchy hair loss in young adults and children. This could cause total baldness or alopecia totalis. Around 90 percent of everyone who has this condition but the hair will come back in a couple of years.

- Androgenic Alopecia

This is a condition that is genetic and can affect women and men. Men who have this condition that we call male pattern baldness could begin losing their hair in their teen or early 20s. It can be seen by a receding hairline with a gradual disappearance of hair from the front of the scalp and the crown. Women who have this problem that we call female pattern baldness won't notice this thinning until they reach their 40s or even later in life. Women will have thinning hair over the whole scalp. The hair loss is most noticeable at the crown.

- Involutional Alopecia

This is a condition that is natural where the hair gradually gets thinner with age. More of the hair follicles will enter into the resting stage. This makes the rest of the hairs get fewer in number and shorter.

Causes of Hair Loss

No one actually knows why some hair follicles have been programmed to have shorter growth cycles than others. There are several factors that can influence the hair loss:

- Diet

A diet that severely restricts calories or protein could cause hair loss. If you aren't getting enough protein, your body might ration out the protein in your body by shutting down your hair growth. This might show up a couple of months after you have stopped eating protein. This is only temporary and can be fixed by increasing your protein. There are numerous sources of protein you can consume.

- Medical Conditions

Anemia, eating disorders, iron deficiency anemia, diabetes, lupus, and thyroid disease could all cause hair loss. Most of the time, once the condition gets treated, the hair will return as long as there wasn't any scarring from follicular disorders, lichen planus, or lupus.

Anemia happens because of an iron deficiency and can cause hair loss. Your doctor can do a blood test to make sure you have anemia. Taking an iron supplement could fix this problem. Other symptoms of anemia might include cold feet and hands, pale skin, dizziness, headache, and fatigue.

Hypothyroidism is basically an underactive thyroid. This small gland that is located in your neck makes hormones that are needed for your metabolism along with your development and growth. If it isn't pumping enough hormones into your body, it can cause hair loss. A blood test can figure out the try cause behind it. When your thyroid has gotten back to normal, your hair should return.

- Cosmetic Procedures

Dyeing your hair, bleaching, perms, and shampooing excessively can cause your hair to thin because it makes the hair brittle and weak. Using hot curlers or rollers, braiding your hair too tight, and running a pick through very tight curls could break and damage hair. These procedures won't cause baldness. Most of the time, the hair will grow back if the cause is stopped. But severe damage to the scalp and hair could cause some permanent baldness.

- Autoimmune Disease

Most autoimmune diseases could cause alopecia areata. This type of baldness causes the immune system to crank up for reasons unknown and can affect the hair follicles. In some of the people who have alopecia areata, their hair will grow back, even though it might be very fine and a lighter color than before. The normal thickness and color will eventually return.

- Age

It isn't uncommon to notice that your hair is thinning once you reach 50 years of age. This type of hair loss can't be treated unless you want to undergo hair transplants. Using scarves and wigs are one way to go.

- X-rays, Injuries, and Burns

Any of these could cause a temporary hair loss. In these cases, your normal hair will return when the injury has healed unless it produces a scar. If this happens, the hair won't ever return.

- Pulling Your Hair

One impulse control disorder called trichotillomania can cause you to pull out your hair. You don't have any control over it, you just constantly pull and play with your hair. This can cause big chunks of your hair to fall out. This normally starts before you turn 17 and is more common in women than men. Some antidepressants could help, but behavioral modification therapy is a better option.

- Drugs

There are specific classes of drugs that can cause hair loss. The most common are beta-blockers that are used to treat blood pressure and some blood thinners. Other drugs that could cause hair loss are antidepressants, ibuprofen, and other NSAIDs, lithium, and methotrexate.

- Childbirth

Any of these could cause some temporary hair loss. Pregnancy is a good example of physical stress that can cause you to lose your hair. This is more common after you have given birth because having a baby is traumatic. If you do lose your hair after you give birth, don't worry because your hair will come back in a few months. Ringworm that is caused by fungal infections could cause some hair loss, too.

- Stress and Illness

Any type of trauma, like an illness, car accident, or surgery, could cause hair loss. This hair loss happens when stress causes the hair roots to be pushed into the resting or shedding stages. This is just temporary, and your hair will begin to grow back once your body recovers.

- Vitamin A

Taking too much vitamin A could trigger your hair loss. The normal daily value for Vitamin A is about 5,000 IU each day. Taking more than 10,000 IU daily could cause you to lose your hair. This is completely reversible. Just stop taking vitamin A.

- Deficient in Vitamin B

This isn't common in the United States; having a deficiency of vitamin B can cause hair loss. Just like having anemia, a simple supplement can fix the problem. You can also change up your diet. Vitamin B can be found in fruits other than citrus, starchy vegetables, meat, and fish. Eating a balance of vegetables and fruits along with "good fats" like nuts and avocado are good for your health and hair.

- Quick Loss of Weight

Losing weight suddenly is a type of trauma that could cause you to lose your hair. This happens even though the weight loss was good for you. The weight loss can put some unnecessary stress on your body. Since you haven't been eating right, it could have resulted in mineral or vitamin deficiencies. Losing your hair and weight might be a sign of eating disorders like bulimia or anorexia. This, too, will fix itself with some time. You will have about six months of hair loss, and then it will come back.

- Genes

If you come from a long line of hair loss, you are going to have it, too. Inheriting genes from both the female and male parent could influence a predisposition to getting female or male pattern baldness.

- Anabolic Steroids

If you are taking steroids to bulk up, you might find that your hair begins to fall out. These have the same impact on your body the PCOS does. Your hair should return once you stop taking the steroids.

- Hormones

Just like the pregnancy hormone can cause hair loss, if you stop taking your birth control pill, this can cause it, too. The change of hormone that happens during menopause could cause the same thing. An abnormal level of androgens, which are male hormones that are produced by both women and men, can cause hair loss. If you have started taking a new birth control pill, talk to your doctor about your hair loss and see if you can either go back to what you were on or see if there is another pill that will work for you.

Signs of Hair Loss

These signs will vary between children, women, and men. But people of any sex or age might notice some more hair being collected in your shower drain or hairbrush.

Some signs of hair loss in men might include:

- A semi-circle shaped pattern that exposes the crown
- Receding hairline
- Thinner hair

Signs of hair loss in women:

- Thinning of the hair especially at the crown

Signs of hair loss in young adults and children:

- Excessive shedding of hair after stress, anemia, rapid weight loss, drug treatments, and illnesses
- Incomplete hair loss or patches of broken hairs on the eyebrows or scalp
- Total loss of hair over all the body
- Sudden loss of hair in patches

When to call your doctor:

- Our child or yourself have suffered an unexplained hair loss on any body part

- Your child is pulling or rubbing out their hair

- Your child has incomplete hair loss or broken hairs on their eyebrows or scalp

- Your child or yourself has a sudden loss of hair in patches

Treatments

There are some remedies that promise to restore hair to a balding head, and some of these have been used since ancient times. Most women and men who have thinning hair can't do much to reverse this process. Most people will turn to weaving, hairpieces, and wigs after they lost their hair from drug treatments or surgery. Some might get a tattoo to simulate eyelashes or eyebrows. There are some drugs that can slow down hair loss, and there are some alternative treatments that can help the remaining hairs' health, but there isn't one treatment that will replace a complete head of hair.

Some people could benefit from these treatments:

- Janus Kinase Inhibitors

This is a class of immunomodulators is showing some promises in the clinical studies that treat alopecia areata

- Lasers

Home-based and office laser devices have been successful in stimulating hair growth.

- Diphencyprone

This is a sensitizing agent that is used topically and only occasionally to stimulate the hair growth for people who have alopecia areata.

- Anthralin or Drithocreme

This is a medication that is used topically to control the inflammation around the base of the hair follicles. It has been used to treat conditions like alopecia areata.

- Corticosteroids

In some cases of alopecia areata, a person's hair loss will resolve itself spontaneously. In most cases of alopecia areata which is an autoimmune disorder, is what causes a person's hair to fall out in clumps. Some doctors will try to speed up recovery by prescribing topical corticosteroids or shots directly in the areas of hair loss. This treatment might be a bit painful and might cause some skin to thin at the injection sites. Prednisone could be effective for alopecia areata, but the side effects could include menstrual problems, acne, metabolic abnormalities, and weight gain. Any positive effects are normally just temporary.

Prevention

Even though there isn't a total cure for balding, you could protect your hair from being damaged and leading to the thinning of the hair.

Most people put a lot of stress on how their hair looks. Chemical cosmetics, hair straightening products, tight braids, permanents, hair dyes, hot curlers, and hair dryers could cause thinning, brittle, and dry hair.

In order to prevent damage to your hair, do the following:

- Brush Right

Brushing your hair properly could do the same damage to your hair as any other product. Using the right brush, apply gentle pressure to the scalp and bring the brush down to the tips of the hair to distribute the natural oils into the hair. You have to work gently and don't brush your hair when it is wet. This is the time when your hair is most fragile. When your hair is wet, you need to use a wide-tooth comb.

- Pick the Right Products

Use a shampoo that is right for your type of hair. If you like curling your hair, pick sponge rollers as they won't damage your hair. Use a natural-bristle brush that is slightly stiff. It won't break or tear the hair.

- Be Natural

Try to leave your hair its natural texture and color. If this isn't an option, give your hair time to recover between chemical treatments or blowouts. Don't tightly braid your hair.

Hair Loss for Women

The easiest way to think about how your hair grows is to compare it to a garden. How well your garden grows, all depends on what happens underground.

Just like a garden, a normal growing cycle should produce a product, which is your hair. Hair growth cycles are important since if they don't work properly, this is a reason we lose our hair.

Chemicals, infection, illness, and medications can interfere with this cycle, and they can stop hair from growing properly.

Even though hair loss might seem more prominent in men, women are just as likely to have thinning or no hair. Most women will see it when they reach their 50s and 60s, but it could happen at any age for many reasons.

- Ways to Grow

As stated above, the hair will grow in three stages: telogen, catagen, and anagen. Around 90 percent of all the hair on your head is in the anagen stage. This can last between two and eight years. The catagen stage usually lasts about two to three weeks. During this time, the hair follicle will shrink. In the telogen stage, the hair will rest. This will last about two to four months.

Most of the time, the hair will be growing. About ten percent of the strands will be in the resting or transition stage at the same time. Hair will grow around six inches each year.

- Losing Hair

Many people will lose about 50 to 100 strands every day. When you wash your hair, you could lose about 250 strands. Don't ever stop washing your hair to try to keep it. It is going to fall out eventually.

For people who don't count their hair each day, there are ways to see if your hair is being lost faster or thinning. Women will notice the difference faster than men. When you wake up each morning, look at your pillow, there might be a large amount of hair on your pillow. Each time you comb your hair, you might notice a large amount being left in the comb or brush.

There are other cues that you could look for. Even though men's hair normally recedes from the crown or forehead, women will notice the thinning on the top half or third of their scalp. Their frontal line normally stays intact. Women might see their part getting wider, or they might see more scalp when they pull their hair back.

There are ways your doctor can make a diagnosis. Blood work will be taken to rule out autoimmune diseases or thyroid problems aren't to blame.

- Genes

There are other ways to diagnose your problem, and that is by listening and looking. Just take some time to look at your ancestors. If some of them have similar or even greater amounts of hair loss, you can expect to look like them one day. Your doctor can use a magnifying glass to look at the scalp to see if your follicles are in different sizes. These are some good signs of female pattern baldness. This is also known as androgenetic alopecia.

This condition is hereditary and affects around 30 million women. It is the most common type of hair loss. It happens in about 50 percent of all women. It normally shows up in their late 50s or 60s, but it could happen any time even as early as their teenage years.

Every time a normal hair follicle is lost, it gets replaced by one that is the same size. Women who have female pattern baldness, the new hair will be thinner and finer. Basically, it becomes a miniaturized version of itself. Your follicles are getting smaller, and they will eventually stop growing.

- Medical Conditions

If all your hair follicles are the same size, or if you have a sudden loss in hair, it is probably caused by something more than just heredity, such as a medical problem.

There are many conditions that could cause hair loss. The most common are anemia, thyroid problems, and pregnancy. Others might include seborrheic dermatitis, psoriasis, PCOS or polycystic ovary syndrome, and autoimmune diseases.

Even though there is a link between hair loss and menopause, there isn't a direct correlation. It might be that hair loss and menopause just happen around the same age. Other reasons might include too much vitamin A, drastic weight loss in a short amount of time, intense illness, surgery, or extreme stress. Hair loss could happen in just a couple of weeks, or it might take six months.

- Take It Easy

Another way that thinning hair is self-inflicted is people who wear their hair in extremely tight braids or cornrows. Everything that a woman does to manipulate their hair, flat irons, blow dryers, bad brushes, chemical treatments could cause breakage and damage. These include too much brushing and aggressively towel drying when your hair is wet.

For most of these problems, the hair will grow back, or the loss could be changed with medical treatments. You need to see a dermatologist if you think something is wrong. The sooner you start treatment, the more chances you will have for improving your hair growth.

Caring for Thinning Hair

You can lose hair for many different reasons. Medicines and illnesses could cause hair loss. Hair loss could be inherited. Usually, the hair will thin due to being fine-textured, or you have used too many harsh chemicals on your hair, and it begins to break easily.

These tips can protect your hair, add volume, and prevent more hair loss:

- Pick a Style that Works for You

Blow dryers aren't a problem if you keep the heat low. Be extremely careful about placing heat onto your hair. Curling irons and flat irons could damage your hair and cause breakage.

- Shampoo Hair When Needed

In order to protect your hair, it is best to only shampoo your hair when it gets dirty. Since fine hair will get dirty faster, people who have fine hair will need to shampoo more often, although fine hair will break easier. Fine-textured hair will benefit from getting a good shampoo and some conditioner that will build volume.

- Use Volumizers

Most hair products that build volume will contain paraffin or beeswax. This isn't good for hair since it can build up and make your hair break. If you buy your products at a salon, they will actually help. They don't damage the hair or weigh it down. You can apply mousse at the roots for some support. You can start blow drying at the roots. Apply some pressure gently with a brush to create some volume. You can use a finishing spray to hold it in place.

How Dr. Sebi Reversed Alopecia

Dr. Sebi has constantly shared all his discoveries about food. He created a program that was found to be "consistent with the African genetic structure." The food he recommends is not hybrids. Hybrid foods need starch to get bound together. Starch is basically an acid.

Dr. Sebi's diet is based on the knowledge that foods could influence our body's pH levels. This means all the foods we eat could make our bodies more basic or more acidic. Because diseases thrive in acidic environments where mucus starts to spread in the body, this will keep oxygen away from our vital organs. He thought that you could reverse this process by getting rid of starch and blood from the diet.

Should you try Dr. Sebi's diet? Well, only you can answer that question. He was a true believer that there wasn't any book that could give you the knowledge that your own experiments and discovery could. Even though he was and is still trusted by many, it is important for you to do your own research before changing your diet. If a diet requires any drastic changes to how you look at food, you need to ask yourself some important questions.

I have asked myself: "If my grandmother has lived for 100 years and is still going strong, and I watch her eat pickled pig's feet, what does this mean for me?"

You have to challenge yourself with some questions that you don't know the answers to. If you think that Dr. Sebi's diet is something that might help you and you want to try it, begin with some baby steps. Do a lot of research online and find support groups. Find some recipes that were inspired by Dr. Sebi and give them a try. If you have to change them up until you get the diet down, that is fine. The main thing is to do your research and listen to your body. This will make your experience better, and it will make you feel more confident in changing your lifestyle.

CHAPTER 5

OVERCOMING LUPUS WITH DR. SEBI

Lupus is a horrible long-term autoimmune disease where your body's own immune system gets hyperactive and begins to attack healthy, normal tissue. Some symptoms can include damage, swelling, and inflammation to your lungs, heart, blood, kidneys, skin, and joints.

Because of its complex nature, some people call lupus the "disease of 1,000 faces."

There are, on average about 16,000 new cases of lupus every year in the United States. There are over one million people who are living with lupus. Lupus normally only affect women and happens between age 15 and 44.

In 2015, lupus gained attention when Selena Gomez announced she was diagnosed in her teen years and had taken treatments for it. Lupus isn't contagious, and it can't be transmitted in any way to another person. There have been some extremely rare cases where a woman with lupus gave birth to a child who developed a type of lupus. This is known as neonatal lupus.

Types of Lupus

There are several types of lupus. The main ones are neonatal, drug-induced, discoid, and systemic lupus erythematosus.

- Neonatal

Most of the babies who are born to mothers who have systemic lupus erythematosus are usually healthy. About one percent of all the women who have autoantibodies that are related to lupus will give birth to a child with neonatal lupus.

The mother might have no symptoms, Sjogren's syndrome, or SLE. Sjogren's syndrome is another condition that can happen with lupus. Most of the symptoms include dry mouth and dry eyes.

If a baby is born with neonatal lupus, they might have low blood count, liver problems, or a skin rash. About ten percent have anemia. The rash will normally go away within a couple of weeks. Some infants will have a congenital heart block. This is when the heart can't regulate a rhythmic and normal pumping action. The baby might need to have a pacemaker. This could be a condition that is life-threatening.

If you have SLE and want to get pregnant, you need to talk with your doctor before and make sure they keep a close watch on you during your pregnancy.

- Drug-induced

About ten percent of all the people who have SLE will have symptoms show up due to a reaction to specific drugs. There are about 80 drugs that can cause this condition.

These could include some drugs that are used to treat high blood pressure and seizures. They might include some oral contraceptives, antifungals, antibiotics, and thyroid medicines.

Some drugs that are associated with this type of lupus are:

- Isoniazid: this is an antibiotic that is used in the treatment for tuberculosis

- Procainamide: this is a medicine that is used to treat heart arrhythmias.

- Hydralazine: this is a medicine that is used to treat hypertension.

This type of lupus normally goes away once you stop taking the specific medication.

- Subacute Cutaneous Lupus Erythematosus

This refers to lesions that appear on the skin that was exposed to the sun. These lesions won't cause any scarring.

- Discoid Lupus Erythematosus

With this type of lupus, the symptoms only affect the skin. Rashes will appear on the scalp, neck, and face. These areas might become scaly and thick, and scarring might happen. This rash could last from a couple of days to many years. If it does go away, it might come back.

DLE doesn't affect any internal organs, but about ten percent of all the people who have DLE will also develop SLE. It isn't clear if the people already had SLE, and it only showed up on the skin or if it progressed from DLE.

- Systemic Lupus Erythematosus

This is the most common type of lupus. This is a systemic condition, meaning that is can impact any part of the body. Symptoms could be anywhere from extremely mild to extremely severe.

This one is the most severe of all the types of lupus because it can affect any of the body's systems or organs. It could cause inflammation in the heart, blood, kidneys, lungs, joints, skin, or a combination of any of these.

This type of lupus normally goes through cycles. During remission times, the patient might not have any symptoms at all. When they have a flare-up, and the disease is very active, their symptoms will reappear.

Causes

We know that lupus is an autoimmune disease, but one exact cause hasn't been found.

What happens?

Lupus happens when our immune systems attack healthy body tissues. It is more than likely that lupus is the result of a combination of your environment and genetics.

If a person has an inherited predisposition, they might develop lupus if they come in contact with something in their environment that triggers lupus.

Our immune systems will protect our bodies and helps to fight off antigens like germs, bacteria, and viruses. This happens because it produces proteins that are called antibodies. The B lymphocytes or white blood cells are what produce these antibodies.

If you have an autoimmune condition like lupus, your immune system can't tell the difference between healthy tissue, antigens, or unwanted substances. Because of this, our immune system will direct the antibodies to attack the antigens and healthy tissues. This can cause tissue damage, pain, and swelling.

An antinuclear antibody is the most common type of autoantibody that develops in people who have lupus. These ANA react with the cell's nucleus. All these autoantibodies are circulated throughout the blood, but some of the cells in the body will have walls that are thin enough to allow some autoantibodies to move through them.

These autoantibodies could attack the body's DNA in the cells' nucleus. This is the reason why lupus will affect certain organs but not others.

Some possible triggers might include:

- Medications: Lupus could be triggered by some blood pressure medicines, antibiotics, and anti-seizure medicines. People who get drug-induced lupus normally get better once they stop the medicine. Symptoms rarely persist after they stop the drug.

- Infections: Getting an infection could cause a relapse or initiate lupus in certain people.

- Sunlight: Being exposed to the sun could trigger an internal response or cause skin lesions in certain people.

Why the Immune System Goes Wrong?

There are some genetic factors that play a role in the development of SLE. Some of the genes in the body can help the immune system to function properly. People who have SLE, these changes could stop their immune system from working right.

One theory relates to the death of cells. This is a natural process that happens as the body renews cells. Some scientists think that because of some genetic factors, the body doesn't completely rid itself of all the dead cells. The cells that are dead and stay in the body might release substances that make the immune system malfunction.

Risk Factors

You might develop lupus due to many different factors. These could be environmental, genetic, hormonal, or any combination of these.

- Environmental

Environmental agents like viruses or chemicals might contribute to causing lupus to show up in certain people who might be genetically susceptible.

Some possible environmental triggers could be:

1. Viral infections: These might trigger some symptoms in certain people who are susceptible to SLE.

2. Medications: About ten percent of most cases of lupus could be related to a certain drug.

3. Sunlight: Being exposed to sunlight can trigger lupus in some people.

4. Smoking: The rise in more cases in the past several decades might be because of being exposed to tobacco.

5. Genetics

Scientists haven't proved that one certain genetic factor can cause lupus, even though it is a lot more common in some families.

Genetics might be the cause of the following risk factors:

1. Family history

Anyone who has a first or second-degree relative who has lupus will have higher risks of getting lupus. Scientists have found specific genes that might contribute to getting lupus. There just hasn't been enough evidence to prove that they actually cause the disease.

In some studies done with identical twins, one twin might get lupus while the other doesn't, even if they did grow up together and have been exposed to the same environmental factors. If one twin has lupus, the other one will have about a 25 percent chance of getting this disease, too. Identical twins are more genetically imposed to have this condition.

Lupus could happen to people who don't have any family history of this disease, but there might be other autoimmune diseases within the family. Some examples include idiopathic thrombocytopenic purpura, hemolytic anemia, and thyroiditis.

Some researchers think that changes to the x-chromosomes might increase the risk.

2. Race

People of a certain background can develop lupus, but it is about three times more common in people who have an African background as compared to Caucasians. It is also more prevalent in Native American, Asian, and Hispanic women.

• Hormones

These are chemicals that get produced by the body. They help to regulate and control activities of certain organs or cells.

This hormonal activity might explain these risk factors:

1. Age

The diagnosis and symptoms usually happen between the ages of 15 and 45, basically, during a woman's childbearing years. But about 20 percent of all cases happen after a woman turns 50.

Since nine out of ten lupus diagnoses are female. Scientists have looked at a link between lupus and estrogen. Women and men produce estrogen, but women do produce more.

In one study done in 2016, some scientists found that estrogen could affect the immune activity and cause lupus antibodies to develop in women who are more susceptible to lupus.

This could explain who autoimmune disease will affect more women than men. During 2010, scientists published a study that reported women who had been diagnosed with lupus reported more fatigue and pain when menstruating. This might suggest that symptoms might flare more during this time.

There just isn't enough evidence that will confirm that estrogen actually causes lupus. If there is an actual link, an estrogen-based treatment could regulate how severe lupus gets. A lot more research is needed before doctors will offer it as an actual treatment.

- Gut Microbiota

Researchers have recently been looking at gut microbiota as one factor in developing lupus. Scientists say specific changes to gut microbiota happened in both mice and people who have lupus. They need more research in this area.

Can Children Be at Risk?

Lupus is very rare in children who are under 15 years of age if their birth mother didn't have it. If their birth mother had it, they might have lupus-related skin, liver, or heart problems.

Infants who have neonatal lupus might have higher chances of getting a different autoimmune disease later in their life.

Symptoms

During flare-ups is when people who have lupus will feel the symptoms. During times between the flare-ups, people won't have any or only a few symptoms.

Lupus has many symptoms, and these include:

- Arthritis
- Purple or pale toes or finger from stress or cold
- Unusual hair loss
- Chest pain when taking deep breaths
- Headaches
- Fever
- Sensitive to sun
- Mouth ulcers
- Skin rashes causedby bleeding under the skin
- Swollen lymph nodes or glands
- Swelling around the eyes or in the legs
- Swelling or pain in the muscles or joints
- Weight loss and a loss of appetite

- Fatigue

Systemic Lupus Erythematosus

This type of lupus can affect people in various ways, and symptoms can happen to different body parts, such as:

- Joints and Muscles
  - o Swollen joints
  - o Arthritisaches and pain
- Blood
  - o High blood pressure
  - o Anemia
- Heart
  - o Atherosclerosis
  - o Inflammation of the fibrous sac
  - o Endocarditis
- Skin
  - o Red or butterfly patches
- Stomach
  - o Severe pain
- Kidneys
  - o Blood in urine
- Lungs
  - o Pulmonary hemorrhage

- o Pulmonary emboli

- o Pneumonitis

- o Pleuritis

- Abnormal headaches

- Nose ulcers

- High fever

- Mouth ulcers

- Hair loss

Effects on Other Systems

Lupus could affect these systems, too:

- Heart

If inflammation reaches the heart, it could cause endocarditis and myocarditis. It could also affect the membrane surrounding the heart, and this can cause pericarditis. Chest pains and other symptoms could result because of this. Endocarditis could also damage the valves of the heart, and this causes the valve surface to thicken. This results in growths that could cause heart murmurs. Lupus could cause inflammation of your arteries, too. The risk of heart attacks and cardiovascular disease will increase a lot.

- Blood

Lupus could cause thrombocytopenia, which is a decrease in how many platelets are in the blood. Platelets help to clot the blood. It can also cause leucopenia, which is a decrease in the number of white blood cells. Lupus could also cause you to be anemic.

- Blood Vessels

The inflammation of blood vessels or vasculitis could happen. This could affect your circulation.

- Central Nervous System and Brain

Lupus could affect your central nervous system or brain. If your brain has been affected by lupus, you might have some symptoms like behavioral changes, strokes, seizures, vision problems, memory disturbances, depression, dizziness, or headaches. Most people who have lupus will experience problems with their memory and might have a hard time expressing their thoughts.

- Lungs

Some people who have lupus might develop pleuritis, which is an inflammation in the lining of the chest cavity that can cause chest pain when breathing. Developing pneumonia or bleeding into the lungs could be possible.

- Kidneys

Nephritis or the inflammation of the kidneys could make it hard for your body to get rid of waste and other toxins efficiently. About one in three people who have lupus will develop kidney problems. Lupus could cause some serious damage to the kidneys. Kidney failure is the main cause of death for people who have lupus.

Other Complications

Lupus can increase the risk of developing many other health problems like:

- Pregnancy

Women who have lupus have a bigger risk of preeclampsia, preterm birth, and miscarriages. Preeclampsia is a condition that also causes high blood pressure. In order to reduce the risk of developing these complications, doctors will recommend delaying getting pregnant until you have your lupus under control for six months.

- Cancer

Having lupus can increase the risk of you developing cancer, but this risk is small.

- Bone Tissue Death

This happens when there isn't enough blood getting to the bone. Small breaks could develop in the bones, and eventually, the bone will collapse. It normally just affects the hip.

- Infection

This becomes more prevalent since both lupus and the treatment for lupus can weaken the immune system. Normal infections include shingles, herpes, salmonella, yeast infections, respiratory infections, and urinary tract infections.

The 11 Criteria

Your doctor will use a standard classification scheme to help them diagnose you. If you meet four out of the 11 criteria, your doctor will consider you might have lupus.

This is the 11 criteria:

1. Positive Antinuclear Antibody: Test for ANA is positive, and you haven't used any drugs that could induce it.

2. Immunologic Disorder: Test shows that there are antibodies to antibodies to cardiolipin, antibodies to Sm, or antibodies to double-stranded DNA.

3. Hematologic Disorder: Test shows that hemolytic anemia is present along with a low platelet count or low white blood cell count.

4. Neurologic Disorder: If you have problems reasoning, thinking, psychosis, or seizures.

5. Kidney Disorder: Tests will show high levels of cellular casts or protein in the urine of a person who has been having kidney problems.

6. Pleuritis or Pericarditis: This is an inflammation that affects the lining around the lungs (pleuritis) or the heart (pericarditis).

7. Non-erosive Arthritis: This won't destroy the bones near the joints, but there is normally effusion, swelling, or tenderness in two or more peripheral joints.

8. Nose or Mouth Ulcers: These are normally painless.

9. Photosensitivity: This is a rash that will appear after you have been exposed to the sun.

10. Discoid Rash: This is a raised red patch on the skin.

11. Malar Rash: This is a butterfly-shaped rash that appears across the nose and cheeks.

This system can miss mild and early cases at times. Not being diagnosed can happen since the symptoms and signs are not very specific. But there are some blood tests that could lead to over-diagnosis since people who don't have lupus could have the same antibodies as people who have the condition.

Diagnosis

Getting a diagnosis can be hard since all the various symptoms might resemble the symptoms of other illnesses. It is also hard since the symptoms and signs will vary greatly for each person. The symptoms and signs might vary with time and overlap those of other illnesses. There isn't one test that can diagnose lupus. Your doctor will ask you about symptoms, do an examination, and take a family and personal medical history. They will take into consideration the 11 criteria that I mentioned above. Your doctor might also request some blood testing along with other laboratory tests.

- Image Tests

If you or your doctor thinks that your lupus is affecting your heart or lungs, they might suggest that you have either:

- o Echocardiogram: This test utilizes sound waves to make images in real-time of your heart while it is beating. This checks for problems with the valves and other parts of the heart.

- o Chest X-ray: This is an image of the chest that might reveal shadows that might an inflammation or fluid buildup in the lungs.

Other image tests could help your doctor to see any organs that are affected by lupus.

- Tissue Biopsy

Your doctor might also request a biopsy. Lupus could harm the kidneys in several ways, and treatments vary depending on the kind of damage that happens. There might be a time when it will be necessary for your doctor to take a sample of your kidney tissue to find out what treatment would be best. This sample gets taken through a small incision or with a needle. Skin biopsies are sometimes done to see if lupus is damaging your skin.

- Urine Test

These can help your doctor diagnose and monitor the effects that lupus is having on your kidneys. They are looking for cellular casts, white blood cells, red blood cells, and protein that could help show how your kidneys are working. For some of these tests, just one sample is needed. For others, the person might have to collect several samples over a 24-hour time frame.

- Blood Tests

This can show if specific biomarkers are present. These biomarkers can give your doctor information about which one of the autoimmune diseases you might have.

1. Erythrocyte Sedimentation Rate

This is a blood test that shows how fast red blood cells settle on the bottom of a tube in one hour. If they settle faster than normal, this might show lupus. This test isn't specific to just one disease. It could be elevated if you have cancer, other inflammatory conditions, an infection, or lupus.

2. Serum Complement Test

This measures how much protein your body consumes when inflammation occurs. If you have low levels, this shows that inflammation is present in your body and that your SLE is active.

3. Anti-histone Antibodies

These are proteins that have a role when creating DNA. People who have drug-induced lupus normally have them, and anyone who has SLE might have them. These won't necessarily confirm a diagnosis.

4. Anti-La/SSB and Anti-Ro/SSA Antibodies

There is about 30 to 40 percent of all the people who have lupus will have anti-La/SSB and anti-Ro/SSA antibodies. These can happen with people who have Sjorgren's syndrome and anyone who has lupus but tested negative for ANA.

They can be present in a tiny amount in around 15 percent of the people who don't have lupus, and it can happen with other conditions like rheumatoid arthritis. If a woman has anti-Ro and anti-La antibodies, there might be a chance that her baby will have neonatal lupus after birth. Anyone who has lupus and wants to get pregnant will need to be tested for these specific antibodies.

5. Anti-U1RNP Antibody

About 25 percent of all the people who have lupus will have anti-U1RNP antibodies. People who don't have lupus will have less than one percent of these antibodies. This antibody might be present in someone who has Jaccoud's arthropathy and Raynaud's phenomenon which is a deformity of the hands caused by arthritis.

6. Anti-Smith Antibody

About 20 percent of all the people who have lupus will have an antibody to Sm, which is a ribonucleoprotein that will be present in the cell's nucleus. It will be present in less than one percent of all people who have lupus. It is extremely rare in people who have other rheumatic diseases. Because of this, anyone who has anti-sm antibodies will likely have lupus, too. It isn't normally present with kidney lupus.

7. Anti-dsDNA Antibody

This is the anti-double-stranded DNA antibody, which is a certain kind of ANA antibody that happens in about 30 percent of everyone who has lupus. Less than one percent of people who don't have lupus will have this type of antibody. If you test positive, it might mean that you have a serious form of lupus-like kidney lupus or lupus nephritis.

8. Anti-DNA Antibody Test

About 70 percent of all the people who have lupus will have an antibody called the anti-DNA antibody. This will normally cause a positive when you are having a flare-up.

9. Antiphospholipid Antibodies

APLs are kinds of antibodies that are directed against phospholipids. APLs will be present in about 50 percent of all the people who have lupus. People who don't have lupus could have APLs, too. Anyone who has APLs could have a higher risk of pulmonary hypertension, stroke, and blood clots. There is also more of a risk of complications during pregnancy including miscarriage.

10. Antinuclear Antibodies

About 95 percent of all the people who have lupus will have positive results when taking the ANA test. Some people who test positive for ANA, but won't have lupus. Other tests will have to confirm this diagnosis.

- Biomarkers

These are genetics, proteins, antibodies, and other factors that will show your doctor what is happening with your body or how your body is responding to treatments. These are useful because they could show that a person has a condition even if they don't have any symptoms. Lupus could affect different people in different ways. This makes it hard to find biomarkers that are reliable. But doing a combination of tests, including blood tests, could help your doctor determine your diagnosis.

- Monitoring Tests

Your doctor will continue to do tests to find out how lupus is affecting your body and how well your body responds to treatments.

Home Remedies and Treatments

There isn't a cure for lupus, but the flares and symptoms can be managed by medication and lifestyle changes. The treatment that your doctor chooses depends on your symptoms and signs. Figuring out whether your symptoms need to be treated and with what medicines need to be carefully considered. Your doctor has to take into account all the risks and benefits.

As your symptoms and flares lessen, your doctor might decide to change your dosage or medicines. These are the medicines that are normally used to control lupus:

- Rituximab

This is beneficial if you have a resistant strain of lupus. Some side effects might be an allergic reaction to the infusion, and an infection could happen.

- Biologics

This is a different kind of medicine. The most common is Benlysta, and it gets administered intravenously. It can reduce the symptoms in some people who have lupus. Some side effects are infections, diarrhea, and nausea. Sometimes depression might get worse.

- Immunosuppressants

These are drugs that suppress the immune system and might be helpful in the more serious cases of lupus. Some examples of this type of drug are Trexall, CellCept, Azasan, and Imuran. Some side effects might include the risk of cancer, decreased fertility, liver damage, and infections.

- Corticosteroids

Prednisone is the most popular type of corticosteroid. These drugs can help with the inflammation caused by lupus. High doses like Medrol or Methapred are used to control serious diseases that damage the brain and kidneys. Some side effects are infections, diabetes, high blood pressure, thinning of the bones, easy bruising, and weight gain. The risk of these side effects will increase with higher doses and longer therapy.

- Antimalarial Drugs

These medicines are normally used to treat malaria-like Plaquenil. These can affect the immune system and could help to decrease flares. Side effects could include damage to the retina and upsetting the stomach. Normal eye exams are recommended when you take these medicines.

- NSAIDs

Taking over the counter NSAIDs like Motrin, Advil, and Aleve can be used to treat fever, swelling, and pain associated with lupus. Stronger NSAIDs can be obtained by prescription. Some side effects include increased risk of developing heart problems, kidney problems, and possibly stomach bleeding.

Treatments try to:

- Reduce organ damage
- Manage or prevent flares

Medications could help:

- Control cholesterol
- Reduce infections
- Manage blood pressure
- Prevent or reduce organ and joint damage
- Balances hormones
- Regulates the immune system's activities
- Reduces swelling and pain

Your exact treatment depends on how lupus is affecting you. If you don't do any treatments, flares can happen that could have life-threatening consequences.

Lifestyle Changes

You need to take steps to take care of yourself if you have been diagnosed with lupus. There are simple measures that can help you prevent lupus flares, and if they do happen, help you cope with the symptoms you have experienced. You need to try to:

- Calcium and vitamin D Supplements

Talk to your doctor about these. There is evidence that suggests people who have lupus might benefit from taking a vitamin D supplement. A 1200 to 1500 mg calcium supplement might keep your bones healthier.

- Eating Healthy

A healthy diet will include whole grains, along with fresh vegetables and fruits. Your doctor might give you some dietary restrictions if you have gastrointestinal problems, kidney damage, or high blood pressure.

- Stop Smoking

Smoking can increase your risk of getting a cardiovascular disease and could make the effects of lupus on your blood vessels and heart.

- Exercise

Make sure you exercise regularly. Exercise can keep your bones strong and helps to reduce the risk of having a heart attack. It can also promote a general well being.

- Sun Smart

Since ultraviolet light can cause a flare, you need to make sure you wear protective clothing like long pants, long-sleeved shirts, and a hat. Make sure you use sunscreen that has an SPF factor of no less than 55 each time you head outside.

- Visit Your Doctor

Make sure you have regular checkups rather than just seeing your doctor when your symptoms get worse. This could help your doctor prevent flares and could be useful when addressing routine concerns like exercise, diet, and stress. This can help prevent complications from lupus.

Alternative Medicine

Some people who have lupus look for complementary or alternative medicine. There aren't many alternative therapies that can change the course of lupus, even though some could help to ease the symptoms.

Talk about these treatments with your health care provider before you try them by yourself. They can help you weigh the risks and benefits and will be able to let you know if they will interfere with your current medicines. Some of the alternative and complementary treatments might include:

- Acupuncture: This treatment uses tiny needles that are inserted just under the skin. This could help ease muscle pain that is associated with lupus.

- Dehydroepiandrosterone or DHEA: Try to find supplements that contain this hormone. It could help with muscle pain and fatigue. It could cause acne breakouts.

Dr. Sebi's Cure for Lupus

Having lupus isn't a joking matter. What makes this disease even worse is the way health care professionals work with lupus patients. Some doctors want to kill your immune system with chemotherapy or begin giving you shots of concentrated starch, which is a lot worse than alcohol. They might as well just put lupus in the same boat as AIDS. The main reason that it hasn't been considered as AIDS is that it doesn't shatter the immune system. The truth of the matter is that for people who have lupus, their immune system is so screwed up that you would be better off not having one. This is why I said it might as well be AIDS.

- What About Lupus?

What has Dr. Sebi taught us about lupus? Your central nervous system has been compromised because there is a yeast infection that no one has addressed right. The cells' mucous membranes are constantly being attacked and turned into pus, and mucus contributes to the cells being deprived of oxygen. Because the cells are exposed and our bodies are stressed with the effort of just trying to function properly, our central nervous system needs some serious help.

- Living Without a Central Nervous System

The life of our cells and nerves that are responsible for sending signals through our bodies have been challenged and diminished as more cells get compromised, and this contributes to more mucus forming in other parts of our bodies. Our bodies are still smart enough to know that it needs to be cleansed since mucus is stopping the cells from doing their job correctly. This will soon keep your organs from doing what they are supposed to do. This causes your pain receptors to go on overload to tell you that something is wrong with the body. Your brain and body want you to quit eating specific foods, and you should know what you need to quit eating. When it seems like your organs don't want to work right, they then start acting like an enemy rather than a friend. Can you guess what your immune system is saying about all this? What do you think your immune system is going to do? It is going to start attacking everything in sight. Now your organs are being attacked. They can't fix themselves anymore, and you can't even get a good night's sleep.

- Why Worry About the Nervous System?

Our bodies need to be able to protect and repair the central nervous system because it helps protect our immune system. They do things at the same time as long as our bodies are producing dopamine naturally. Our bodies can instinctively and immediately protect themselves by sending out phagocyte cells to protect and defend it. It already has these cells place throughout our bodies. Phagocyte cells called neutrophils are what begin attacking your organs. This causes them to die and turn into pus or mucus. We have more of these cells in our bodies than any other kind of phagocytes. These stationary cells called macrophages will begin eating right where they are at. They are only following orders, and they don't know what is good and what is bad. Pain receptors begin going off. But they aren't finished yet. Our central nervous system has some tough guys in the blood. They are called our "natural killer cells." Just imagine what is going to happen when these get confused about who their enemy is? These cells patrol the lymphatic and blood systems, just trying to find any abnormal cells. They will kill off healthy cells faster than they can erode away.

- You Now Have a Compromised Central Nervous System

Your body is confused, and your immune system sets off a fever so that your metabolism gets faster trying to repair everything quickly. This fever begins attracting histamines to areas that have been damaged so they can help call the phagocytes. Now, your body feels as if it has the flu. By this time, the immune system is using the fever to help heal; it is also calling the bones to help trigger leukocytosis. This is when the bone marrow begins producing more neutrophils to help fight. Now, while all this is happening, guess who was supposed to be making sure that everything is being done correctly and that the right enemies have been found: your lymphatic system.

Your lymphatic and immune systems are one and the same. It is supposed to clean up the dirty cells and make them all clean and new. If it fails to do this, your blood pressure is going to drop, your lungs will fill with fluid, your ankles are going to start swelling, and your body just wants to give up and die. It isn't able to do its job correctly once the central nervous system has been compromised.

- How to Handle Lupus?

You get rid of it the same way you get rid of AIDS, cancer, and tumors. You use the Bio-mineral balance along with Intra-cellular chelation. These require you to eat an extremely strict diet. Intra-cellular chelation just means that you are going to clean your cells; every single cell that makes up your central nervous system and organs. You won't just be cleaning your organs but every single cell that makes the organ. Why do you need to do this? If you have cancer present in your body, it is telling you that you have a high level of acid in the body. This is a very high level of mitosis. Mitosis is a cell that eats the tissues and organs. This happens when there is a presence of acid. We have to nourish every part of our bodies at the same time. Disease requires us to nourish our bodies back to health. We need to give them Bio-mineral Balance. This along with the Intra-cellular chelation, will bring our bodies back to the way they were before.

So, what exactly are we going to do:

- o We give our bodies electric cell nutrition

- o We get rid of the mucus

- We stay away from foods that create mucus, hybrid foods, synthetic sugars, and starches

- We fast

Support and Coping

If you have been diagnosed with lupus, you are probably going to have a lot of painful feelings about your disease from extreme frustration to fear. There are challenges to living with lupus that can increase the risk of mental health problems like low self-esteem, stress, anxiety, or depression. To help you cope, you can try:

- Connecting With Others

You can try talking to others who have lupus. You can find people through message boards, community centers, and support groups. Other people who have lupus could give you unique support since they are facing the same frustrations and obstacles that you are facing.

- Time for Yourself

You can cope with the stress by taking time for yourself. Use this time to write in a journal, listen to music, meditate, or read. Find an activity that will renew and calm you.

- Get Support

Find support from your family and friends. Talk about your lupus with family and friends and explain how they could help you when you have flares. Lupus is a frustrating disease for loved one since they can't feel or see it, and you might not look like you are sick.

- Educate Yourself

Write down all the questions you have about lupus when they come to mind so you can ask your doctor during your next appointment. You can ask your nurse or doctor for reputable sources for more information. The more you know about your disease, the more confident you are going to feel about your treatments.

Your Appointment

When you see your health care provider, they might refer you to a specialist to get a diagnosis and for your treatments for any immune disorders and inflammatory joint problems.

Since lupus symptoms mimic other health conditions, you might need to have some patience while you are waiting on your diagnosis. Your doctor has to rule out other illnesses before they diagnosis lupus. You might need to see many specialists like a neurologist, hematologist, or nephrologist. It all depends on what symptoms you are experiencing.

Things You Can Do

Before you go to your appointment, write down answers to these questions:

- What supplements and medications do you regularly take?

- Have your siblings or parents been diagnosed with an autoimmune disease or lupus?

- Have you noticed any specific things that trigger your symptoms?

- When did the symptoms start? Do they go away and come back?

You might want to write down some questions for your doctor like:

- Do I need to see a specialist?

- Are there any restrictions I need to adhere to while waiting for a diagnosis?

- Are there any lifestyle changes that could help my symptoms right now?

- What type of test are you recommending?

- If these don't point to a specific cause, what other tests am I going to need?

- What are some of the causes of my condition or symptoms?

- I am thinking about getting pregnant. What do I need to do? Are there certain medicines that I can't use if I am pregnant?

Never hesitate to ask any question that might pop into your mind while you are at your doctor's office or if there is something they bring you that you don't understand.

What to Expect from the Doctor

Your doctor is going to ask you a lot of questions. You need to be ready to answer them. This will leave you plenty of time to go over the things you want to spend time on. Your doctor could ask:

- Do you plan on getting pregnant, or are you pregnant?

- Do you have any other medical problems?

- Do your symptoms limit your ability to function at home, work, or school? How much do they limit you?

- Are you having problems concentrating or with your memory?

- When you are in the cold, do your fingers get uncomfortable, numb, or pale?

- Do you get rashes when you are out in the sun?

Outlook

People who were diagnosed in the past normally wouldn't survive more than five years. Now, treatment could increase their lifespan. Effective therapy helps you manage lupus, so you can live a healthy, active life. As researchers learn more about genetics, doctors hope they will soon be able to find lupus in earlier stages. This makes it easy to prevent complications before they actually happen. Some people decide to join clinical trials because this can give them access to different medications.

CHAPTER 6

HOW TO HEAL KIDNEY DISEASES WITH DR. SEBI

Your kidneys are two organs that are about the size of your fist that are located near the bottom of your rib cage. Each kidney will be on either side of the spine. In each kidney, there are millions of tiny things called nephrons. These nephrons filter the blood.

You need your kidneys in order to have a healthy body. Your kidneys filter out all the impurities in the blood, excessive water, and waste products. All these toxins get stored in the bladder and then removes them through the urine. Your kidneys regulate the potassium, salt, and pH levels in your body. The kidneys also produce hormones that can control red blood cell production and helps regulate blood pressure. Your kidneys create a type of vitamin D that can help your body absorb calcium better.

Kidney disease will attack these nephrons. The damage it causes might leave the kidneys unable to get rid of the waste. There are about 26 million people in the United States who are affected by kidney disease. This happens when the kidneys get damaged and aren't able to function properly. This damage might be caused by different long-term chronic conditions, high blood pressure, and diabetes. Kidney disease could cause other problems such as malnutrition, nerve damage, and weak bones.

If it gets worse with time, the kidneys might completely stop working altogether. This means that you might have to undergo dialysis to help the kidneys perform. Dialysis is a medical treatment where a machine purifies and filters the blood. This won't cure the disease, but it does help prolong life.

Causes and Types of Kidney Disease

- Urinary Tract Infections

UTIs or urinary tract infections are infections caused by bacteria that occur in any part of the urinary tract. Infections in the urethra and bladder are the most common. These can be easily treated and don't normally cause other health problems. If they are left untreated, they could spread to the kidneys and could cause kidney failure.

- Polycystic Kidney Disease

This is a genetic disorder that creates many cysts that grow inside the kidneys. Cysts are just small fluid-filled sacs. These can cause kidney failure and create problems with how the kidneys function. Kidney cysts are common and usually harmless, but polycystic kidney disease is different and a more serious problem.

- Glomerulonephritis

This is an inflammation in the glomeruli. These are very small structures in the kidneys that filter the blood. This disease could be caused by congenital abnormalities, drugs, or infection. It normally gets better by itself. Congenital abnormalities happen right after or during birth.

- Kidney Stones

This is just one more normal kidney problem. This happens when substances like minerals crystallize in the blood within the kidneys. These form stones or solid masses. These are normally expelled from the kidneys during urination. Passing these stones is very painful, but they don't usually cause many problems.

- Chronic Kidney Disease

This is the most common type of kidney disease. This is a condition that is long-term that won't improve with time. It is normally caused by chronic high blood pressure.

This is very dangerous for your kidneys since it increases the pressure in the glomeruli. These are small blood vessels inside the kidneys where the blood gets cleaned. With time, pressure on the vessels can damage them, and then your kidney function starts to go downhill.

With time, chronic kidney disease can damage the glomeruli and nephrons. It can cause other problems with the kidneys like infections, stones, cysts, and cancer.

Your kidney function will continue to deteriorate until the kidneys can't do their job properly. This is when you would need to begin dialysis. This helps to filter out waste and extra fluid from the blood. This can help treat your kidney disease; it just won't cure it. Getting a kidney transplant might be another option. It all depends on the circumstances.

Diabetes is the main cause of getting chronic kidney disease. Diabetes is numerous diseases that can cause high blood sugar. Having a high level of sugar in the blood can damage the blood vessels with time. This means that your kidneys won't be able to clean the blood properly. Kidney failure could happen when your body gets overloaded with toxins.

Symptoms of Kidney Disease

This disease could easily go unnoticed until your symptoms get too severe. The following is a list of early warning signs and symptoms that you could be getting kidney disease:

- Late-night urination

- Scaly, dry skin

- Puffy eyes first thing each morning

- Swollen ankles and feet

- Muscle cramps

- Poor appetite

- Sleeping problems

- Problems concentrating

- Fatigue

The following are severe symptoms that might mean your disease is getting worse and turning into kidney failure:

- Pericardium becoming inflamed

- Elevated potassium level

- Low sex drive

- Anemia

- Fluid retention

- Changes in how much urine your body expels

- No appetite

- Vomiting

- Nausea

Risk Factors

People who have diabetes do have a higher risk of getting kidney disease. This is the main cause of kidney disease. It accounts for around 44 percent of all new cases. You are more at risk of developing kidney disease if you:

- Are of Native American, Asian, Hispanic, or African descent

- Are elderly

- Have a family history of chronic kidney disease

- Have high blood pressure

Diagnosing Kidney Disease

Your doctor will be the first to know if you are in a high-risk group for getting kidney disease. They will do some tests to see how well your kidneys are functioning. Some of the tests might be:

- Blood Creatinine Test

This is a waste product that gets released into the blood if creatine gets broken down. How much creatinine is in the blood increases when the kidneys don't function properly.

- Urine Test

Your doctor will ask for a sample of urine to test it for albumin. This is a protein that gets passed into the urine if the kidneys become damaged.

- Kidney Biopsy

When doing a kidney biopsy, your doctor will take out a little piece of tissue from the kidney after you have been sedated. This sample could help determine if you have kidney disease, what type you have, and the amount of damage that has already happened.

- CT Scan or Ultrasound

A CT or computed tomography scan and ultrasound can give your doctor clear pictures of your urinary tract and kidneys. These images let your doctor see if your kidneys are too large or small. They can also any structural problems or tumors that might be there.

- GFR or Glomerular Filtration Rate

This test measures to see how well the kidneys work and shows what stage of kidney disease you might be in.

Treating the Disease

Treating kidney disease will focus on controlling what caused the disease. Your doctor can help manage your cholesterol, blood sugar, and blood pressure levels. They might use some of the following to help treat your kidney disease:

- Lifestyle and Dietary Changes

Changing your diet is just as important as taking your medications. Learning to live a healthier lifestyle could help prevent a lot of the causes of kidney disease. Your doctor might suggest you:

o Lose some weight

- o Exercise more

- o Stop smoking

- o Lower your alcohol consumption

- o Begin a healthy diet that includes whole grains, fresh vegetables, and fruits.

- o Lower your salt intake

- o Lower your consumption of high cholesterol foods

- o Take insulin injections

Dialysis

This is an artificial way of filtering the blood. This gets used when your kidneys are very close to failing or have completely failed. Most people who have kidney disease might have to go on dialysis totally or until you find a kidney donor.

There are two kinds of dialysis: peritoneal and hemodialysis.

- • Peritoneal Dialysis

In this type of dialysis, the peritoneum starts functioning for the kidneys. The peritoneum is the membrane that outlines the abdominal wall. A tube gets implanted and is used to fill the stomach with dialysate. All the waste in the blood will flow out of the peritoneum and into this dialysate. This fluid then gets drained out of the stomach.

There are two types of this dialysis:

- o Continuous cycler-assisted peritoneal dialysis: for this one, a machine is used to pull the fluid in and out of the stomach while you sleep.

o Continuous ambulatory peritonealdialysis: for this one, the stomach is filled and then drained numerous times throughout the day.

The common side effects are infection of the stomach cavity or around the area where the tube was inserted. The other side effects could include hernias and weight gain. A hernia happens when a part of the intestine pushed through a tear or weak spot in the stomach wall.

- Hemodialysis

For this type of dialysis, your blood is pumped into a special machine that will filter out fluid and waste. This can be done at a center, hospital or home. Most people will have this done three times each week. Each session will last between three and five hours. Hemodialysis could be done in more frequent, shorter sessions.

A few weeks before you begin hemodialysis, your doctor will do surgery to make arteriovenous fistula. This gets created by connecting a vein and an artery just under the skin. It is usually done in a person's forearm. This large blood vessel that the doctor created lets a larger amount of blood to continuously flow during treatments. This means that more blood could be purified and filtered. The doctor might implant a looped plastic tube which is called an arteriovenous graft and use it for the same purpose of they can't join a vein and artery together.

The side effects of this type of dialysis are itching, muscle cramping, and low blood pressure.

Outlook

The bad news is that once kidney disease is diagnosed, it won't go away. The best way to maintain your health is to follow your doctor's advice and adopt a healthier lifestyle. Kidney disease could get worse with time. It could even cause kidney failure. This could be life-threatening if you leave it untreated.

Kidney failure happens if your kidneys aren't working at all or if they are just barely working. This can be managed through dialysis. As stated above, this involves a machine being used to filter the waste from your blood. Your doctor might recommend you have a kidney transplant.

Preventing Kidney Disease

There are some risk factors that you can't control, like family history, race, or age. There are things you can do to help prevent kidney disease:

- Stop smoking if you smoke

- Lower your salt intake

- Control your blood pressure

- If you have diabetes, control your blood sugar

- Drink lots of water

Watch OTC Drugs

You have to be careful when taking over-the-counter drugs. Always follow the dosing instruction on the label. If you take ibuprofen or aspirin, it could lead to kidney damage. If the normal dose of these medicines don't control your pain, call your doctor.

Be Tested

If you are worried about your kidneys, ask your doctor about being tested. Kidney disease doesn't normally cause any symptoms until they are more advanced. The standard blood test called a BMP, or basic metabolic panel can be done during any routine exam. This can show any early problems with your kidneys. They can be treated easier this way. If you have high blood pressure, heart disease, or diabetes, you need to have a test done every year.

Limiting Specific Foods

There are various chemicals in foods that can cause some types of kidney stones. These could include:

- Oxalate: this is a chemical found in chocolate, sweet potatoes, spinach, and beets

- Citric acid: this can be found in any citrus fruits like grapefruits, lemons, and oranges.

- Animal protein like chicken and beef

- Too much sodium

Calcium Supplements

Don't take a calcium supplement before you talk to your doctor first. Some supplements can actually increase your risk of kidney stones.

Dr. Sebi's Cure for Kidney Disease

Basically, any problem with your kidneys might lead to your blood not being purified well. This causes toxins to be accumulated in the blood. You might have a family history of kidney problems, high blood pressure, and diabetes. Recent studies show that overusing normal medications for various diseases can play a huge role in deteriorating the health of your kidneys. Many people are habitual users of medications, even for the slightest aches and pains. You have probably done it since you didn't know that these drugs could harm your health including your heart, liver, and kidneys. Many people today have moved to a more holistic approach for their health. Dr. Sebi knew what some scientists are trying to prove today. He might have known that people today would need his help in curing their kidney problems. Yes, he created a herbal remedy for kidney problems.

If you have been diagnosed with kidney disease, following Dr. Sebi's diet can help you. Make sure you talk with your doctor if you feel like something isn't quite right with your health. When you think about all the toxins being put into our bodies today, it isn't any wonder that there are so many people with kidney problems.

Ingredients in the Kidney Disease Kit

Dr. Sebi's kit combines many very healthy and rare herbs that he thought was perfect for any kidney problem. Unfortunately, not all problems can be treated with the same herbs. Dr. Sebi's kits let you customize them for your needs. Let's look at the ingredients:

- UTI Special Mix: UTIs are the most common problem with kidneys. If you are constantly getting UTIs, this might help you stop getting them.

- Kidney Stone Hunter: This herbal mix works against kidney stones. Even if you don't get kidney stones, this can help detoxify your body.

- AHP Zinc Powder: AHP or ayurvedically herb purified zinc powder can be taken by anyone who has a zinc deficiency. Zinc deficiency can cause kidney problems.

- Swarna Bang Tablets: This combination of herbs has been used for thousands of years to fight recurring UTIs. These are strong enough to help the kidneys, too.

- Chandanadi Tablets: This herbal combination includes Daruharidra-Berberis aristata, sandalwood oil, karpoora, rala-shorearobusta, amalaki, acacia catechu, kattha, gandhabirojasatva, sugandhamaricha, and sandalwood. These herbs are combined in the correct proportion to get the perfect outcome.

- Punarnava Special Kidney Mix: Some reports published about kidney disease claims panarnava is one herb that help the kidneys function properly.

Benefits

As you know, your kidneys are a critical filtration part of your body. Without it, we wouldn't be able to survive for long with all the toxins we are exposed to everyday. Even the slightest of imbalances in filtering out toxins, we could be faced with problems like cysts, kidney stones, UTIs, gout, or other chronic and severe complications. Some are fairly common, but others can be life-threatening.

Dr. Sebi's kidney kit gives your body the minerals and herbs your body needs to keep your kidneys healthy. They can help your body function better by detoxifying your body. The herbs help to cleanse the kidneys of all the toxins it has stored up. This won't happen overnight; it will take several months for you to notice any results. Each kit will last for about two months.

When you go to Dr. Sebi's website, there will be some questionnaires for you to feel out. These will help them pick the right combination of herbs for you. You will then get to decide what you want to try in order to improve your health.

CHAPTER 7

DR. SEBI NUTRITIONAL GUIDE

Here is a complete guide to the best foods that you should eat while following Dr. Sebi's diet.

Seasonings and Spices

- Date sugar
- Pure agave syrup
- Powdered granulated seaweed
- Pure sea salt
- Sage
- Habanero
- Onion powder
- African bird pepper
- Cayenne
- Achiote
- Thyme
- Tarragon
- Sweet basil

- Savory

- Oregano

- Dill

- Cloves

- Bay leaf

- Basil

Oils

- Avocado oil

- Hempseed oil

- Sesame oil

- Grapeseed oil

- Coconut oil

- Olive oil

Seeds and Nuts

- Brazil nuts

- Walnuts

- Tahini butter

- Sesame seeds (raw)

- Hemp seeds

Grains

- Wild rice

- Tef

- Spelt
- Rye
- Quinoa
- Kamut
- Fonio
- Amaranth

Herbal Teas

- Tila
- Raspberry
- Ginger
- Fennel
- Elderberry
- Chamomile
- Burdock

Fruits

- Tomatillo
- Tamarind
- Soursops
- Soft jelly coconuts
- Raisins
- Prunes
- Prickly pear

- Plums
- Plum tomatoes
- Pears
- Peaches
- Papayas
- Oranges
- Olives
- Melons
- Mango
- Limes
- Grapes
- Figs
- Dates
- Currants
- Cherries
- Cherry tomatoes
- Cantaloupe
- Elderberries
- Berries
- Bananas
- Avocado
- Apples

Vegetables

- Wild arugula
- Purslane
- Watercress
- Zucchini
- Turnip greens
- Squash
- Sea vegetables
- Onions
- Okra
- Nopales
- Mushrooms
- Kale
- Izote
- Garbanzo beans
- Dandelion greens
- Cucumber
- Chayote
- Bell peppers
- Amaranth greens

Things to Remember

- Never eat seedless or canned fruits.

- Don't ever use a microwave as it can "kill" the food.

- All Dr. Sebi's products will release their properties two weeks after you take them.

- Most of the grains listed above can be found as cereal, flour, bread, or pasta. Most stores carry them now. If not, you should be able to find them in any health food store.

- Most grains are alkaline-based. You should only eat the grains listed above rather than wheat.

- Never consume alcohol, hybrid foods, fish, dairy, or animal products.

- You should follow the above guide to the letter. Take any Dr. Sebi products on a regular basis for the best results.

- Any Dr. Sebi product can be taken at the same time without any interactions.

- You should take all products one hour before you take your medications.

- Drink one gallon of water each day.

- If there is a food that you normally eat that isn't listed above, stop eating it immediately as it isn't recommended.

CONCLUSION

Thank you for making it through to the end of *Dr. Sebi Treatment and Cures Book*, let's hope it was informative and able to provide you with all of the tools you need to achieve your goals whatever they may be.

The next step is to decide what changes you are going to make right now. What problems do you need to heal? Do you have diabetes or an auto-immune disorder? Maybe you aren't suffering from any of the diseases mentioned in the book, and you simply want to make sure you never develop any of them. Whatever reason you chose to purchase and read the book is your reason, but you need to start taking steps towards beginning Dr. Sebi's diet and treatments. The best places to start is by studying the nutritional guide, and continue to do your own research on what Dr. Sebi products you should start using.

Finally, if you found this book useful in anyway, a review on Amazon is always appreciated!

DESCRIPTION

Are you looking for a new way to get healthy? Do you wish there was a way to overcome health problems without the damaging effects of modern medicine? If you answer yes to either of these questions, then Dr. Sebi is who you need.

Dr. Sebi was a Honduran herbalist and healer who discovered that a simple diet could be the cure for so many illnesses in the world. This book is here to provide you with the various treatments Dr. Sebi created, and the best thing is, they are all super similar and closely related. Nearly everybody in the world is faced with some sort of health problem, some worse than others. Many of the health problems don't even have a cure in the modern medicine world.

Think about the number of auto-immune diseases there are, such as HIV and lupus. Doctors don't know how to heal those diseases. All that is available are medicines to help control them, which is great, but wouldn't it be great if there was something you could do that would get rid of the disease altogether? Dr. Sebi wanted that, and that's what he did.

His diet and treatments didn't focus on weight loss, but instead, it focuses on healing the body as a whole. It doesn't just focus on one thing. Today, most people simply see his diet as an alkaline diet, and while it is, his philosophy is what sets him apart. This book has been created to share with you his treatment philosophy for some of the most common diseases people are faced with. Within these pages, you will learn:

- How Dr. Sebi's treatment plan can help STDs like herpes and HIV

- The reason why eliminating mucus can help with diabetes

- Why hair loss no longer has to be permanent

- Dr. Sebi's nutritional guide

- Who Dr. Sebi is and his treatment philosophy

… And much more.

Understand that this may seem all too good to be true, or that it's telling you modern medicine is completely bad. You will find that Dr. Sebi never tells you to stop taking medicines prescribe by doctors. Instead, you will use his diet, products, and treatments, along with your doctor's orders to help you heal.

And I'll be honest with you, it won't be easy. It will take some willpower to cut out the foods that you need to for your health. But, with the information in this book and your own desire to become healthy and heal your body, I am certain you can do it.

Right now, it's up to you to make the final decision. Stay exactly as you are right now. Fed up with how you feel, and unable to do anything about it, or buy this book and make changes your body will love you for. Go ahead, scroll back up and click "buy now."

EXTRA CONTENT:

EXPLORE THE COLLECTION OF BOOKS ABOUT DR. SEBI

I wrote this collection in order to reach as many people as possible the knowledge of Dr. Sebi. Do a lot of studies and extract all the information that can lead a person to experience a real change in their life, in a simple way. Here is a preview of what you will find in the rest of the books and you will be able to empirically experience the benefits of following his teachings in a complete way.